Discovery Science

Explorations for the Early Years
Grade K

David A. Winnett

Robert A. Williams

Elizabeth A. Sherwood

Robert E. Rockwell

Innovative Learning Publications

Addison-Wesley Publishing Company

Menlo Park, California • Reading, Massachusetts • New York
Don Mills, Ontario • Wokingham, England • Amsterdam
Bonn • Sydney • Singapore • Tokyo • Madrid • San Juan
Paris • Seoul • Milan • Mexico City • Taipei

This project owes its success to the hard work of the parents, students, administrators, and teachers of the Edwardsville, Illinois, Community Unit School District Number 7.

Project Editor: *Mali Apple*
Production Manager: *Janet Yearian*
Production Coordinator: *Claire Flaherty*
Design Manager: *Jeff Kelly*
Cover and Text Design: *Christy Butterfield*
Photographs: *Bill Brinson*

This book is published by Innovative Learning Publications™, an imprint of the Alternative Publishing Group of Addison-Wesley Publishing Company.

ISBN 0-201-29063-4
1 2 3 4 5 6 7 8 9 10-ML-97 96 95 94 93

This Book Is Printed
on Recycled Paper

Acknowledgments

A sincere thank you to the teachers of the Edwardsville, Illinois, Community Unit School District Number 7 who volunteered their time and talent to assist us in field testing the activities in this book: Nita Ahola, Carol Aljets, Lynda Andre, Mary Ellen Borchers, Sheila Bowens, Jane Bradford, Betty Brazier, Patty Brinson, Bernice Brown, Lori Burns, Nora Cooper, Gail Cullen, Missy Dietzel, Marian Dowdy, Sheri Dreyer, Gloria Fayollat, Harriet Ford, Chris Garbe, Joanie Green, Boots Gullicksrud, Lesley Hangsleben, Beth Jennings, Barbara Kinsella, William Macdonald, Judy Maxon, Mary May, DeAnne McConnell, Tonya McKinney, Kay Morgan, Judy Payne, Carmen Pineiro, Connie Pival, Linda Pokorny, Nancy Schofield, Virginia Small, Debi Stapleton, Connie Vaitekunas, Shirley Ward, Kathy Weber, and Cathie Wright.

We also acknowledge the help given to us by Sally Parker at Brentnell School, Columbus, Ohio and Suellen Girard at Thomas Jefferson School, Alton, Illinois.

Special thanks to Christine Norris and Laura Holloway, our graduate assistants, for numerous hours of observation and data collection; Ann Scates, Science Resource Center coordinator, for typing and organizational expertise; and Sharon Winnett, for sharing her language development and early childhood expertise, as well as her constant encouragement, throughout this project.

And finally, our greatest thanks to the children who gave us instant feedback about what did and did not work.

Dedication

To children, teachers, and parents: We hope Discovery Science will support your interest in science and the excitement of discovery.

Thank you Sharon Lee, David, and Erin for so willingly and lovingly accepting the simple lifestyle of a classroom teacher's family and encouraging me to do what I love to do so much: teach kids about science.

D. A. W.

I wish to thank all the staff at the Rivers Curriculum Project and M. L. for understanding when I had to "go write." To my family: Katie and Clarence in Montana, Sissy and Shawn in Florida, JoAnn and Wally in North Dakota, Jeff and Blanca in California: I love you all.

R. A. W.

To Don: Thank you isn't a big enough word. To Tom, my brother, and Terry, the sister I always wanted. Your love and support mean so much to me. To Jennifer and Will, two remarkable people, for sharing their love and their joy in discovery with me. I am proud to be your mother.

E. A. S.

To Donna, my wife and friend; my daughters, Susan and Janet; my grandchildren, Teri, Robert, Amanda, Kathryn, and Michael; and my mother, Erma Lee.

R. E. R.

CONTENTS

UNIT 4: PLANTS   205

. . . the scientifically literate person is one who is aware that science, mathematics, and technology are interdependent human enterprises with strengths and limitations; understands key concepts and principles of science; is familiar with the natural world and recognizes both its diversity and unity; and uses scientific knowledge and scientific ways of thinking for individual and social purposes.

—Science for All Americans,
American Association for the Advancement of Science

INTRODUCTION

What Is the Focus of Science for Young Children?

Discovery Science visualizes children as learners actively constructing knowledge rather than passively taking in information. Through their individual activity, children form knowledge and make it their own. They come to the educational setting with diverse backgrounds and experiences. It is essential that science, mathematics, and literacy skills be part of an integrated curriculum that recognizes and builds from this diversity.

The goals that follow are the foundation for building a successful early childhood science learning system—a system cognizant that the ultimate responsibility for learning lies with the learner; a system allowing that each learner is different and unique; a system enabling children to fulfill Jean Piaget's goal of education: "To create people who are capable of doing new things, not simply repeating what other generations have done—people who are creative inventors and discoverers."

Goals for Early Childhood Science

1. To promote the development of fundamental problem-solving skills

2. To promote personality dispositions indicative of good scientific problem solvers

3. To promote awareness of careers in science, mathematics, and technology

4. To raise children's comfort and confidence level with science through conscious efforts to counter bias against science

5. To promote development of a knowledge base of basic scientific principles and laws, providing the foundation upon which a clear and accurate understanding of the world can develop. A solid foundation reduces the risk of children acquiring misconceptions that may hinder later their understanding of more complex science concepts

6. To provide an environment that supports active discovery

Why Is Empowerment So Important?

We define empowerment as follows: To allow a person the sense of power to make decisions and to take actions on one's own volition. Discovery Science's inquiry model begins by asking children: What do you know? This is followed by Free Discovery (where children explore materials on their own), followed by asking: What did you learn? followed by experiences developed and structured for children to ask questions and to seek their own answers. Children are *empowered* to become scientists.

This sense of empowerment frees children to seek information and answers based on their own curiosity. They should be able to see science as a way to investigate the world and realize that science is all around them. Because children are natural inventors, they take delight in thinking, making, and doing. As they begin Free Discovery, they are taking the first steps toward the development of technological ability. Making and doing requires them to raise questions, thus building the structural base for later scientific thinking.

Why Is the Curriculum Built Around Only Four Units?

Often textbooks are packed too full of science concepts and terms that children are expected to absorb during the brief school year. For most young learners, this is far too much in too little time. A hurried, brief exposure to science may fail to provide the opportunity for the rich conceptual development that is possible with a more coherent, thoughtful approach. In keeping with the guidelines of Project 2061, Discovery Science presents only four science content areas. This enables children to be totally immersed in the science processes they are developmentally capable of mastering.

We support the view of quality over quantity. When learning is centered around a small number of core concepts, the learner can spend enough time with the materials and concepts to master them. Let's look at adult learners.

Fred and Maria have enrolled in a craft class. In the first session they are introduced to working with stained glass; they practice cutting glass and learn to connect the pieces. They come to the second session ready to learn more. Instead they are told that the class is moving on to ceramics. They learn a little about ceramics and are excited about creating something new. They come to the third session ready to continue with ceramics. The clay is gone. It has been replaced with equipment for wood carving. Instead of acquiring skills, Fred and Maria are acquiring frustration.

Too often, this is what we do to children by moving them quickly from one topic to the next. We subtly teach them to be satisfied with incompetence. With a limited number of topics, children have more opportunities to experience feelings of competence and mastery.

How Does Discovery Science Support Emerging Language and Literacy Skills?

Language is the bottom line in all that we teach. Without strong language skills, children will not be good readers, speakers, decision makers, or problem solvers. Children learn the most about the world around them by actively engaging in their environment. Couple that with exposure to the language of their environment, and they will begin to understand and internalize that language.

We are concerned with three types of language development: receptive, expressive, and semantics. *Receptive language* consists of understanding words as they are spoken to the listener. *Expressive language* is using words to communicate. Such language develops as children are exposed to language in their environment. As teachers we use words we want children to learn, and label items for children as we talk about them.

The most important stage of language development is *semantics*. This means that a person understands the meaning of a word and can use it appropriately. Listen to children as they talk with you and to each other to learn whether they have a real understanding of the words they are using. Children grow in their understanding of new words through both hearing and using them.

Discovery Science provides many opportunities for working with language and literacy. Language is a vital means by which concepts are explored and developed. As children share ideas and observations with each other both verbally and symbolically, they will be using a variety of language skills.

As educators we should allow children to share what they know in whatever way they can and to use that sharing as an opportunity to enhance communication skills. In this context Discovery Science will

- improve effective use and expansion of vocabulary as children seek to describe their observations and to share their discoveries
- allow children to devise their own ways of documenting their experiences
- include group experiences that will model diverse uses of language

- familiarize children with the process of asking a question and looking for an answer, a process often confusing to young children
- introduce alternative methods of communication, such as drawings, charts, and graphs
- focus on effective communication and interesting and accurate content rather than spelling, grammar, and neatness
- encourage sharing and collaboration, which require meaningful oral and written communication

Discovery Charts

Children will collaborate with each other through small groups and whole-class discussions, often through informal conversation. Sometimes you will structure the interaction by using Discovery Charts, lists of "what we know," to periodically record what children know and to give direction to class planning. Discovery Charts communicate to children: What we are doing is important enough to write down and remember.

Many variations on the basic Discovery Chart are used throughout the units. You should use Discovery Charts at the beginning of each unit to assess children's current level of understanding. Suggestions specific to each topic are included in the unit introductions. Make additions to Discovery Charts whenever significant new information is generated. You may draw attention to added information in a variety of ways. When much new information needs to be recorded, you may want to prepare a separate chart. If you are adding only a few concepts, write them in a different color. This will emphasize to children, and to families who see the Discovery Charts on the wall, that more information is being acquired.

Review the Discovery Charts with the children often. This not only reinforces the science concepts but also supports emerging literacy skills. At times children may realize that a statement written earlier is not accurate. For example, an early Discovery Chart may state that magnets pick up metal. Through Free Discovery, children will discover metals that a magnet will not pick up. When children become aware of the discrepancy between their earlier statement and their current knowledge, help them create a new, more accurate sentence. Writing it in a different color will help emphasize growth in learning.

Save and reread these charts later in the year, long after work on a unit is complete. This review conveys the value and consistency of the information that the children have acquired.

Discovery Journals

Discovery Journals, a key component of Discovery Science, are blank booklets children use to document their explorations. They are a means of communicating with others and a permanent record of what they have learned that they can share with their families. It is a rewarding experience for children to look back at their beginning entries to see their own progress.

Children are introduced to the process of recording their discoveries in the first unit. Early entries may consist of something as simple as a drawing with a brief caption, or a few dictated comments. The entries will become more complex as the children grow in skill level and understanding, and expand to include charts, graphs, and other documentation of the children's science learning.

Make separate Discovery Journals for each unit. The simplest way to make journals is to staple several sheets of blank paper between two sheets of construction paper. Recycled paper works just fine. Have children decorate their own covers.

Science Vocabulary

The Science Vocabulary in each activity is the specialized vocabulary that children need to know semantically to fully understand the science concepts they are exploring. We encourage you work with the children to develop "operational" definitions for the words introduced. The operational definition for a word is simply the meaning children derive that fits well with their own ongoing exploration of the concepts. This idea of seeking a more relevant definition for word meaning encourages children to use language freely.

An example will help clarify the concept of operational definitions. During the piloting of the unit on magnets, a small group of children was exploring what a magnet would and would not attract. One girl, acting as spokesperson for the group, explained the way a magnet works. "On one end is the magnet and the other end is metal." At this point in their investigations, the children had come to understand operationally that a magnet is an object with a magnetic end and a metal end. If magnets attract metal and if magnets attract each other, then one side must be the magnet and the other side metal.

The class had done no work with polarity at this point. It would have been inappropriate for the teacher to have jumped in and corrected the child's definition. Through later investigations this group of children came to understand that both ends of a magnet will attract metal and that therefore both ends are magnetic. Think of the discouraging implications for Free Discovery if the teacher had interrupted with, "No, this is how a magnet works. . . ."

We are trying to give children the confidence to explore and discover on their own—to have power over the direction their inquiry may follow. Misconceptions can be corrected through additional experiences rather than through verbal correction of the semantic understanding of the words.

How Does Discovery Science Tap into Mathematics?

Integrating mathematics with science is necessary for several reasons. Mathematics is a significant part of the language of science. Mathematical understanding is an essential component of a child's ability to communicate scientific discovery. And measurement and basic arithmetic skills are needed to quantify observations. Science discovery and investigation provide the perfect opportunity for children to apply graphing, charting, and data-analysis skills to real problem-solving situations.

In Discovery Science, children have a chance to learn science and mathematics skills together as part of a unified curriculum. Showing children the connection of numbers to practical examples from science enables them to begin to operationalize mathematical skills—increasing the chances that they will understand and appreciate mathematics as adults.

What Is Free Discovery?

Children have a need to know. Free Discovery is observation and exploration at children's own pace, a means to support their curiosity about the natural and physical environment in which they live. Having the freedom to explore at their own rate, without fear of getting "wrong" answers, is critical. In a secure and comfortable environment, children fulfill their natural eagerness to find possible solutions to their own inquiries of why, what, how, and when in their own way. To accomplish this, Free Discovery should

- allow children to become familiar with the materials
- allow children to make observations and discoveries on their own and to feel good about them
- build children's self-esteem through their being in control of their own actions
- provide no right or wrong answers, and therefore no failure
- provide a nonthreatening learning time
- proceed at each child's own learning pace

The Role of Free Discovery

To be most effective, science programs must emphasize inter-action with the environment, both natural and social. By providing simple equipment and materials, we give children unlimited opportunities to explore and interact without set parameters. This can be difficult for adults, who often want to intercept children's natural and spontaneous curiosity with questions and challenges that are adult- rather than child-initiated. Children are often not ready for such interruptions. Free exploration and play are a need that must be fulfilled before children can see the materials as learning resources.

As adults we have simply learned to complete this learning process more quickly than children because of our experience and knowledge base. How do we as adults approach learning a new skill? Suppose that you would like to make a table but have never done any woodworking. Do you go buy some wood and some tools and get to work? No, you begin with Free Discovery. You may ask for some help from someone who has a bit more experience. Maybe you read about woodworking. You practice with the tools on wood scraps, not prime walnut. The surer you become of your skills, the more you are able to experiment and modify your techniques. With persistence you eventually learn enough to build the table that you want. This slow flow of learning, moving from inexperience to experience to modification, is a natural process for the adult learner. It is also how children learn when they are given the opportunity.

In Free Discovery and in the activities that follow in Discovery Science, you and the children have specific roles.

The Role of the Teacher

- To encourage children to explore and experiment independently
- To create an atmosphere conducive to learning
- To introduce new ideas, materials, and procedures
- To encourage inquiry and creativity
- To model inquiry, questioning, and problem solving
- To model safe practice
- To provide sufficient materials, information, and space for learning
- To support developmentally appropriate activity
- To assess and evaluate children's learning

The Role of the Children

- To care for and function independently in the Discovery Center
- To understand that they are in control of their actions
- To feel good about discovery
- To cooperate with other children
- To collect data and document activities
- To explore with materials and ideas
- To realize that answers are not right or wrong but simply the results of inquiry
- To communicate about their experiences

How Do I Help Children Focus Their Observations?

The Focusing Observations activities following Free Discovery allow teacher-directed quality control over the types of observations children are making. Children are recording these observations in their minds. Later they can call up an observation and fit it into a larger conceptual framework that allows them to make sense of what they are doing or learning.

You have two major instructional concerns during Focusing Observations activities. First, there are observations about each content area that children need to make. If these observations are not made, children will not begin to understand the concepts. Second, children are continually making inferences about what they have observed. Some of these inferences are correct, and some may not be.

Focusing Observations activities focus children's observations on specific aspects of each concept. Frequently you will ask children to quantify—measure—their observations to make them more precise. You will ask them to isolate various factors that affect their subject and to alter them to make new observations regarding the effect these changes have. For example: a magnet will attract paper clips in air, but what will happen if the paper clips are in water?

Children will become increasingly familiar with the process of making and recording observations. You will be able to assess their understanding of science concepts through the Discovery Journals and classroom discussion by the accuracy and completeness of their observations.

How Do Children Observe to Classify?

Observing to Classify activities follow Focusing Observations activities. Classification is an important skill for children to develop. Young learners naturally want to group and organize objects, and you probably will observe children classifying prior to these activities.

The simplest form of classification takes place when children start to collect similar objects and materials and assemble them together. Encourage this behavior by asking children to verbalize: Why are you putting all of these objects in the same place? Children's responses will likely indicate that a certain attribute has been identified and that the selections are based on that attribute. These children are well on their way to becoming skilled classifiers and will learn additional classification skills quickly. Children who are not displaying the initial desire to group and organize must be given special attention.

The Observing to Classify activities for each unit direct learners to develop increasingly more sophisticated skills. The initial activities ask children to repeat what they have probably been doing on their own: grouping objects according to a single attribute or physical property. To increase the difficulty level of the classification scheme, you later ask children to rank-order objects according to an increase or decrease in the magnitude of a specific property (for example, height, mass, or length).

Eventually you ask children to divide a group of objects by a particular attribute and then to further separate them into groups based on a second attribute. This final classification requires a child to hold two concepts in mind. For example, a child might first divide a group of plants according to height, tall plants and short plants. Then the learner might separate these two groups according to odor, those that have a strong smell and those that do not.

Encouraging children to make use of their observations reinforces the importance of becoming good observers. Classification provides children with an opportunity to make decisions and to be in control.

How Do I Help Children Organize and Communicate Observations?

Organizing and Communicating Observations activities follow Observing to Classify activities. Free Discovery, Focusing Observations, and Observing to Classify are the initial skills that children need to begin establishing order in their world. Your task is to encourage children to make meaningful drawings in their Discovery Journals and to create charts and graphs to help them describe their observations. They will come to understand the need for orderly record keeping and systematic analysis of information—at their level, of course. In addition children will see that much of what they are learning about numbers and simple arithmetic is quite useful in scientific discovery.

Whether in chart, graph, or narrative form, children will come to understand the importance of communicating in a clear manner. Several examples of charts and graphs are shown in the activities.

How Does Discovery Science Involve Families?

As the child's first caregiver and teacher, a family has both the right and the responsibility to be involved in the child's formal education. The interaction will foster a mutual respect between the home and school and result in the growth and understanding of scientific knowledge in the children. Inviting families to become partners in working together for the benefit of the children provides a vehicle through which families and educators can work hand in hand toward the acquisition of scientific literacy for all children.

Discovery Science is an excellent instrument to bring about such involvement. The team effort is encouraged by the spirit and intensity of working together, which is the heart of its potential success. By working together with this curriculum, you can empower all players—teacher, child, and parent—in ways that promise higher levels of scientific achievement.

The Role of the Family

- To encourage discovery by the children
- To model inquiry and problem solving
- To resist answering and solving discovery activities before the child has done so
- To enjoy doing science activities with the child
- To feel free to communicate with the child's teacher, to ask questions, and to seek additional information when needed
- To listen to and give information to the child, always remembering that it is all right for any participant to make mistakes or to say, "I don't know"
- To willingly share available resources from home, such as animals, plants, or soil samples, to be used for Discovery Science activities

Family Connection Activities

There are four Family Connection activities for each unit, simple activities for children to do at home with their families. The activities include a simple set of directions and a list of materials (most often one or two items). Family Connection activities do not introduce new concepts; they reinforce what the children are learning at school. They empower children by giving them the opportunity to share their knowledge and expertise with their families. Put the directions and materials into a resealable plastic bag as a mini-kit for each child to take home.

Additional Ideas for Family Involvement

Introducing Discovery Science: A Family Meeting

This hands-on meeting invites families to be a part of Discovery Science. You will talk with families about Free Discovery and child-initiated learning, encourage them to share materials and expertise, and give them the opportunity to interact with the materials their children will be using. After attending, families will be more adept at both supporting and modeling Discovery Science. Plans for a family meeting, including a sample invitation and flier, planning checklist, and sample meeting format, are in the Family Connection section at the back of this book.

Discovery Science Newsletter

A Discovery Science Newsletter can be a separate newsletter or a portion of a general newsletter designed to keep families informed of science-related school and community activities.

Family Letters

Send a letter home to families at the start of each Discovery Science unit to introduce the topic and to ask for family support and ideas for resources. Sample letters are included in the Family Connection section.

Science-o-Grams: Discovery Notes

Brief notes can update the families on current activity, remind them of an upcoming field trip or event, or tell them about their child's recent discovery.

Family Volunteers

Discovery Science can provide opportunities and access for families to volunteer both at school and at home. Family volunteers can enrich the learning process and expand the learning environment for children as they share skills, personal expertise, and the enthusiasm of discovery. A person does not need a high educational level to share love and knowledge of gardening or information about a pet. Families who might be uncomfortable volunteering in more traditional school roles may find their niche in Discovery Science.

What Is the Discovery Center?

Science with young children can and should be done in almost any setting, just as science and its technological applications permeate the lives of adults. The intention of the science center concept is to begin to develop the idea that although science is everywhere, a well-organized and well-maintained science center provides a good focus for a successful science program. The Discovery Center is the site for Free Discovery and other child-administered activities, and also serves as the storage site for materials to be used elsewhere.

The size and organization of your classroom will determine the Discovery Center's total area. Consider how many children you would like the Discovery Center to accommodate at one time.

Because children work largely on their own, the Discovery Center promotes problem solving and positive risk taking. Children learn to make independent decisions as they explore concepts designed to teach the how-to of science rather than words and facts. The Discovery Center

- belongs to all the children
- provides ample materials in an accessible way
- serves as a resource and library
- provides a safe and orderly place to work
- sets the stage and mood for exploration

Discovery Center Materials

Materials in the Discovery Center should be sturdy, simple, and easy to handle. If space does not allow for a permanent center, select materials that can be set up quickly and stored easily. The Discovery Center should contain the following basic equipment:

- safety goggles
- paint aprons or smocks
- magnifying devices such as hand lenses, bug boxes, tripods, and two-way magnifiers
- double-pan balance

- spoons, scoops, droppers, and forceps
- containers such as bowls, bottles, margarine tubs, and cups
- sorting and storage containers such as egg cartons and clear plastic vials with lids
- cardboard or plastic foam food packaging trays for sorting and mess containment
- nonstandard units for measuring length and mass, such as animal counters, large metal washers, Unifix® cubes, and interlocking cubes
- Discovery Journals and other writing materials
- cleanup equipment, such as buckets, sponges, paper towels, dust pans, and hand brooms
- large sheets of newsprint for charts

In addition, you will need to add other materials for each unit. These materials are listed in the introduction for each unit.

Setting up the Discovery Center: Storage and Management

Children need plenty of freedom, time, equipment, and materials—properly cared for and stored in areas accessible to them—to become thoroughly involved in discovery. Storage space must be thoughtfully designed to meet each classroom's instructional needs. Several types of storage are necessary. Some materials, such as magnifiers, paper, and a balance, should be out and available at all times, promoting their use and encouraging children to find new functions for them. Shelves, tables, and pegboard are useful for this type of storage.

Some materials must be stored out of the way until needed. Plastic storage tubs that are sold in discount stores have lids, come in a variety of sizes, and stack easily, allowing whole sets of materials to be stored together. The availability of clear lids and a variety of colors increases their flexibility. They can be made available to children or stored out of reach.

Other materials must be available but not necessarily out on open shelves. Resealable plastic bags are useful for small sets of materials. Small tubs, boxes, and crates are also helpful.

Regardless of the size and shape of your storage space and containers, they should be easy to clean and label, inexpensive, and easy for children to use and keep in order. Labeled shelves, racks, hooks, and storage closets can help. As you develop your Discovery Center, also consider the following:

- Clutter-free surfaces for work areas.
- Places on shelves, tables, or the floor to leave materials for an extended time or study.

- The area should be easy to clean. A tiled floor is much more convenient than a carpeted floor. Cleanup materials should be readily available. Responsibility for accidents, along with normal messes, is part of science training.
- Water available either from a sink or special containers is desirable but not always necessary. Water in the area means less traffic to the water taps in the bathrooms.

Caring for Materials

The equipment and materials used in Discovery Science have be selected with children in mind. For the most part they are sturdy, durable, and require the same care as other classroom materials. Some items, such as magnets, need to be stored in a particular way. Special care or storage requirements will be described when such materials are introduced, and this information should be shared with the children.

Maintaining a Safe Discovery Center

The materials used in Discovery Science were chosen because they are inherently safe. We want the children who use these materials to be safe and to develop good safety habits. Safety and learning in the science area begun in the early years can lead to rewarding experiences later in school. A level of comfort with science makes careers in science and related occupations a more likely choice. To establish a safe science area, you must

- model appropriate and safe behavior
- provide a safe place for children to work
- provide a way for children to work without overcrowding
- provide the special information necessary when equipment, materials, or situations might cause a problem

Discuss safety rules each time a new material is introduced. Set clear limits regarding appropriate and inappropriate behavior to enable children to handle and interact with the materials safely. Your concern for safety, however, should be moderated by your good sense and control. Children must be protected, but they also need the chance to try things out as they engage in Free Discovery.

Rules for the Discovery Center must be few, simple, and easy to follow. A well-planned and managed center makes this possible. You must decide what is appropriate for your group and your teaching style.

Enriching the Classroom Environment

The classroom becomes a more powerful place for learning when it has been enriched with books, encyclopedias, magazines, posters, bulletin boards, pictures, card sets, and games. It allows you to expose children to things you cannot bring into the classroom.

Discovery Science encourages experiences with real things, but you cannot bring the entire world into the classroom. Children will learn to expand their knowledge through the use of resource materials. Before you begin each unit, visit the library to select appropriate materials. Beautiful films and videos can be valuable, especially for the Animals unit.

How Do Assessment and Evaluation Fit into Discovery Science?

Assessment is a general term, with a variety of connotations for different groups of educators. The most widely accepted use of the word is in reference to tests used to collect information. Such information can be used by decision makers for the evaluation of individual children or an entire educational program.

Unfortunately the words *assessment* and *evaluation* conjure up visions of child and teacher confrontations and often are viewed as an afterthought to instruction and learning. Pencil-and-paper tests are often inappropriate and inadequate. For the assessment and the resulting evaluation of early childhood science to be of practical value, you must use a somewhat different approach.

The assessment and evaluation procedures used in Discovery Science are consistent with sound test and measurement approaches. They have been developed to be practical and informative for an early childhood teacher in the classroom setting. Assessment and evaluation in Discovery Science is tied closely to instruction and is embedded in the learning cycle, eliminating many of the ill effects of a "tacked on" caboose at the end of the train. Several train engines are placed throughout the long line of cars, engines that will give power and purpose to learning activities.

What Is Authentic Assessment?

As educators we are interested in improving children's skills and expanding their knowledge of the world. To be sure our efforts in education are actually accomplishing the intended purpose, we need to monitor children's development continually. Ongoing educational assessment should be consistent with the instructional approach being used in the classroom and not an inappropriate, high-stakes assessment measure so foreign to the way children process information that it creates frustration and stress.

When assessment measures are tied closely to curriculum and the instructional approach used in the learning environment, we say that it is *authentic*. Discovery Science uses authentic assessment measures in such a way that both teachers and children perceive the assessment as an extension of the learning process.

The assessment system used in Discovery Science has six components: the Success in Science Inventory, curriculum-embedded assessment, Checkpoint Activities, Additional Stimulation Activities, Discovery Journals, and Discovery Charts.

Success in Science Inventory

The Success in Science Inventory, or SSI, is a checklist used to record children's dispositions toward scientific inquiry. When certain behaviors or choices are made by a child, we begin to formulate an understanding of the level of interest and enthusiasm that child has for discovery. Although the SSI may be used at any time in the curriculum, we recommend that you use it during each unit's Free Discovery period to assess the children's interaction with materials and with each other. Evaluate each child at least once in the four units. The suggested levels of performance are: Not apparent, Emerging, and Developed. A scale of 1 to 3 is suggested to simplify scoring.

The SSI will give you a picture of how the class is progressing overall. You will know that Discovery is successful when these early science dispositions emerge among the children. You also will get a feel for when it is time to move on to the next phase of Discovery Science. The children will show that they are ready to do more.

The SSI assesses four science dispositions:

1. The child manipulates objects for useful observations.
2. The child seeks a clear understanding of the questions who, what, where, and when—the facts.
3. The child seeks reasons: asks the question why and tries to answer it through further exploration.
4. The child communicates the results of observations and investigations.

Success in Science Inventory

Child's Name	Science Dispositions				Comments
	1	2	3	4	

1. Manipulates objects for useful observations.
2. Seeks a clear understanding of the question who, what, where, when—the facts.
3. Seeks reason. Asks the question why and tries to answer it through further explorations.
4. Communicates the results of observations and investigations.

Follow these guidelines for using the SSI:

1. Administer the SSI during each Free Discovery session. You may elect to observe and record dispositions for all children each time or to select certain children at different times.

2. Observe and record children's behavior in each of the four science disposition areas.

3. Indicate with a check mark when a child has exhibited a particular disposition. The more marks a child receives, the greater the indication of success in science.

Curriculum-embedded Assessment: Assessing the Activity

Assessing the Activity is found at the end of each activity. Assessing the Activity is a formative evaluation that provides ongoing information about how successfully children are mastering skills and understanding concepts. If children are not able to meet the expectations of the task, you can act immediately to guide them toward better or more accurate understanding of the concepts. You may want to keep a record of these formative evaluations for each child in individual portfolios.

Checkpoint Activities

After children complete a series of activities, they do a Checkpoint activity. The Checkpoint activity is a summative look at how well children have developed the desired skills. Although not to be considered a final unit test, the Checkpoint activity does provide you with an opportunity to observe the children's level of skill mastery. If children have performed well on the Assessing the Activity evaluations, they should have little trouble completing the Checkpoint activity.

Additional Stimulation Activities

If some children find the Checkpoint activity or any of the other activities in the section difficult, the Additional Stimulation activities that follow some Checkpoint activities may be helpful. Children who were not successful with one approach often benefit by working from a completely different perspective. Additional Stimulation activities approach the information in a new way, providing children with another opportunity to learn. The activities are interesting and challenging enough that even children who have mastered the skills will want to participate.

Discovery Journals

The single most important thing to remember when you use children's Discovery Journals for assessment is that they belong to the children. They are the children's own records of exciting learning and discovery. Letter grades, happy or sad faces, or teacher comments written on their pages will quickly eliminate the children's spontaneity, their sense of ownership, and the pride and improvement in skill that comes from self-assessment.

Use the children's journal entries for your own information about what skills and concepts children have grasped and what needs reinforcement. Journals also provide you with a concrete record of each child's development in both science and emerging literacy. You might want to keep completed journals in each child's portfolio.

Discovery Charts

When created at the beginning of a unit, Discovery Charts can serve as a preassessment. They tell you what the class as a whole already knows and can make you aware of misconceptions. When you take the time to refer back to an old chart, to add to it, or to create a new one, children will see that they are learning.

Discovery Charts also can be used as a part of individual assessment. They contain the main body of knowledge generated by the children themselves. Each child should have an understanding of most if not all of the information they contain.

Magnets

Essential Information

Magnets have been used for thousands of years. Early civilizations discovered a rock that attracted smaller pieces of the same rock. This rock, magnetite, also was called lodestone and has been reported in early Greek, Roman, Chinese, and Indian writings. Lodestones opened up the oceans to early explorers: they could be used to restore the magnetism in the primitive compasses on long voyages.

These simple compasses were created by laying a long piece of magnetized iron on a cork floating in a wooden bucket filled with water. Columbus used such compasses to guide his ships across the Atlantic. The processed iron of that day was crude and required remagnetizing every few days. Early experimenters discovered that they could make an new magnet by stroking a piece of iron with a known magnet a number of times in the same direction.

Magnets are classified into three categories. A *permanent magnet* retains its magnetic properties for a long time. A *temporary magnet* is formed when an iron-containing object comes into contact with a permanent magnet. The object will be magnetic for a short time or only while touching another magnet. An *electromagnet* is formed when an electrical current is sent around an iron or steel object. An electromagnet is also temporary, magnetic only when electricity is available.

The poles of a magnet are areas where concentrations of field lines enter or leave a magnet. The poles behave as if they were centers of force. Experimentation will show that poles are present in all magnets. Bringing these poles together produces two distinct outcomes: repelling or attracting. The bar magnets found in most schools are labeled with north and south poles and usually are painted red (north) and white (south). Every magnet has such poles; on donut magnets, the poles are on the flat portion.

Although the effects of magnetism have been known for thousands of years, modern scientists still do not know what causes magnetism. Magnetism and magnetic fields can be determined and described, but the reason for the physical phenomena is unknown. Explanation of the nature of magnetism is given as a unique arrangement of the atoms in metal that contains iron. When such metal is magnetized, all the atoms in the piece line up in the same direction (a *domain* is formed), creating a magnetic

Science Concepts

The following science concepts will be addressed in the Magnets Unit:

1. Magnets attract objects made of metal but not all metals.
2. Magnetic force can pass through various materials.
3. The strength of magnetic force varies.
4. Magnets have poles; like poles repel and unlike poles attract.

field. Dropping, heating, and time cause the arrangement of atoms to change and the magnet to loose strength. The earth is a magnet because the core is composed of domains of iron atoms that are aligned to form a huge magnet. Most planets that humans have studied have a magnetic field similar to that of the earth.

Magnets hold paper to refrigerators, close doors, drive toys, pick up scrap steel, and drive trains across the countryside. The mysteries of the magnet may power the industry and commerce of the next century. Young children should experience the attraction of the magnet, a complex yet very simple phenomenon.

CARE OF MAGNETS

Magnets must be properly cared for and correctly stored. Magnets are weakened by dropping, heating, or improper storage. Avoid sharp blows to or dropping of magnets. Never store magnets in a random manner, such as throwing them into a drawer. Properly store magnets as follows:

- Lay bar magnets in pairs, north pole to south pole.
- Store horseshoe magnets with an iron or steel keeper placed across to connect the two poles.
- Stack round ceramic or flat magnets one on top of the other.

Use a magnet board to conveniently store donut magnets. Many high schools and some colleges have an electric magnetizer that can remagnetize bar and horseshoe magnets.

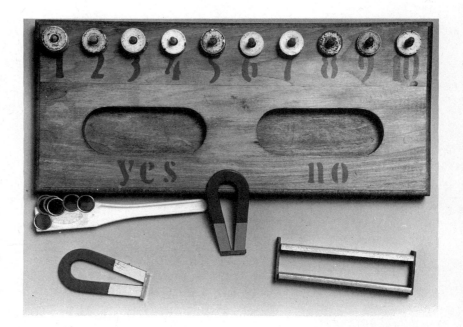

As in all the units, a diversity of materials encourages a greater depth of experience for the children. In addition to these supplies, collect as many different kinds of magnets as you can. Many inexpensive toys and advertising devices use magnets. You can find magnetic drawing boards, magnetic tape, and refrigerator magnets. A great source of unusual magnets is a television or sound system repair shop. Speakers contain very powerful magnets. A repair person may be willing to remove magnets for you from nonfunctioning equipment. Small donut magnets can be purchased in large quantities inexpensively at electronics supply stores.

Collect a variety of materials that are attracted to magnets. Such things as a bag twist with a metal wire inside will surprise the children when it is attracted. Such surprises will broaden their understanding of magnetic attraction.

You may want to send a letter to families to announce the Magnets unit (see the Family Connection, page 284, for an example).

FREE DISCOVERY

Magnets are widely available and come in a rich variety of shapes and sizes. Magnets and other materials that are used in the magnet activities are easy to manage and store and are safe to use. The most important reason for using magnets for the first Free Discovery activity, though, is the pure excitement and interest they stimulate in children. This will be the first time the children have experienced Free Discovery, so extra time for each step of the process will be needed.

What to Do

1. Gather the children into a group. Talk with them about the proper care of magnets and about other new materials they will be using at the Discovery Center. Show each piece as you talk. Pass around some of the materials for them to inspect. Stress safety and cooperation during their investigations.

2. When you have all materials back and the group is ready to listen, make a Discovery Chart. Tape the newsprint to the wall. Ask: What do we know about magnets? Write this question on the paper, with their responses below. Encourage all children to get involved with this discussion. A few probing questions might be useful in stimulating their ideas and discussion; for example, ask: What shape are magnets? and What does a magnet do? If children present misinformation, include it without correction. You will be providing experi-

Getting Ready

Add the following materials to the Discovery Center:

- horseshoe magnets
- bar magnets
- wand magnets
- other magnets, such as magnetic letters and refrigerator magnets
- assorted objects attracted to magnets, such as washers, nuts, bolts, and nails
- assorted objects not attracted to magnets, such as pennies, plastic twist ties, and buttons
- paper clips
- 10-by-10-cm squares of materials such as cardboard, aluminum, plastic, and fabric
- large dishpan or water table
- small boxes with lids
- string or yarn
- 25 painted donut magnets
- 25 unpainted donut magnets
- self-adhesive notes (Post-it™ notes)
- small plastic disks with metal rims (bingo markers)
- straws
- modeling clay
- magnet board (see the photograph on page 22)
- magnet-strip chart (see the photograph on page 55)
- 30 plastic foam balls, 10 each in each of 3 colors
- thumbtacks

Materials

- large sheet of newsprint (for a Discovery Chart)
- markers
- tape
- magnet materials
- Success in Science Inventory (see page 17)
- Discovery Journals

ences later that will allow children to correct misconceptions themselves. This chart will allow both you and the children to see that additional information is acquired throughout the unit.

3. When children have run out of ideas and comments, say something like: Look at all we already know about magnets. Read the list aloud for the children, carefully repeating each of their comments. Stress the importance of their involvement in the discussion. They should feel that their comments are valuable and need to be shared with everyone. They should come to understand that they all belong to one big discovery team and together, through cooperation, they will learn a lot about magnets.

> What We Know About Magnets
> Chad - You can stick it to things.
> Aleta - They are shaped like horseshoes.
> David - They are powerful.
> Hoa - Magnets stick together.
> Matt - Magnets are hard.

4. Introduce children to the idea of the Discovery Journal, the notebook used to record the results of their investigations.

5. Begin Free Discovery. Be sure all children have an opportunity to explore and investigate. During this time they will begin making inferences about magnets and how they work. They need these initial inferences, although they may be incorrect, to start understanding how the world is set up. You need them to make these inferences so that you know where they are in their understanding and can move them farther along. Encourage them to record their findings in their Discovery Journals. Urge them to use pictures, words, or any type of entry their particular stage of communication allows. Later they will use these entries to discuss the question: What did we learn about magnets?

6. Monitor the activities at the Discovery Center. Watch what children do, listen to what they say, and review with them the information they are recording in their Discovery Journals. Be excited about their discoveries.

7. Record individual performance using the Success in Science Inventory.

8. Bring the children back to the discussion group. Remind them to bring anything they have recorded to share their discoveries. The topic this time is: Now what do we know about magnets? Add the new information to the Discovery Chart in a different color. As with all steps of Discovery Science, be a part of this discussion and share what you learned. This will model to them the type of comments you are now soliciting. Invite them to share their drawings and writings. Have them tell you what they discovered. Read over the previous information with the children. Does anything need to be changed or modified? Ask: What else would you like to learn about magnets?

After completing the discussion, you will have a list of their observations and a feel for the kinds of inferences they are making. Now is the time to start focusing their observations about magnets. The loose structure will help you guide them into observations and discoveries that will support or correct the inferences they have made during Free Discovery.

STORY TIME

Use this story-telling activity to raise the children's interest in magnets.

Moving Magnets

This is a story of a lonely little girl named _____ . The reason _____ was so lonely was that she didn't have any friends. You see, she and her parents were constantly moving. They would just get settled into their new home, _____ would start school, and then away they would move to another town. She never stayed anywhere long enough to make friends. She was rarely at a school long enough for the teacher to remember her name!

As a result, _____ became quieter and quieter. And she became fascinated with magnets. She had all shapes and sizes of magnets. She put magnets on her refrigerator and stove, she had her mom and dad stick them all over the dashboard of their car, and she had magnets in the pockets of all her clothes. Now you might think this was a bit unusual, but _____ loved to watch the magnets work. She liked picking up objects around her houses and stacking the magnets together. _____ never showed her magnets to any of the children or teachers in the schools she attended. The magnets were her secret friends.

Then _____ moved again and started going to another new school, but the teacher in this school was not like any teacher she had ever met. This teacher learned her name right away and _____ loved the way she said it. And do you know what else?

This teacher had magnets all over the room, and she had a discovery center that had more magnets than _____ had ever seen! What a great place this was! _____ still didn't talk to the other children or show anyone her magnets.

One day before school when all the children were playing and laughing with each other, _____ saw her teacher arrive. She was loaded down with books and bags and a huge can full of something! All of a sudden, the teacher dropped the can and hundreds of nails spilled all over the playground. The other children just kept running and playing—no one helped the teacher. Quietly _____ came over, bent down with one of her magnets, and began to pick up the nails her teacher had spilled.

One by one, the children come over to watch her. "How do you do that? Where did you get such a great magnet?" some children asked. "Let us help," said another. Soon _____ was laughing and talking with the children as she shared her magnets. Before long, all the nails had been picked up. Best of all, _____ had friends, friends who thought magnets were just as much fun as she did.

_____ was so happy! And guess what else? When she went home that day her mom and dad said they were never going to move again. What a great day it had been!

ACTIVITY 1

Magnet Sorting

Materials (per pair)

magnet

egg carton

set of twelve assorted objects (see
Before the Activity)

This activity asks children to focus their attention on the visual
characteristics of objects attracted to magnets. Egg cartons give
them a way to organize their thinking actively while doing an
easy and often replicated task.

Before the Activity

Prepare sets of twelve objects for classification, including some
that are attracted by a magnet and some that are not. The objects
must be small enough to fit into the compartments of an egg carton. On the inside of the lid of each egg carton, write Yes on one
half and No on the other.

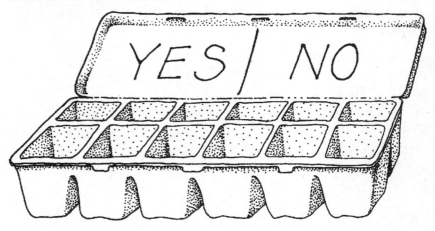

C • O • N • N • E • C • T • I • O • N • S

To Language

Expressive Language - Children will use the science
vocabulary with each other as they work together.

Written Language - Children will differentiate between
the words *yes* and *no*.

To Math

Grouping - Children will divide a collection of objects
into two distinct groups.

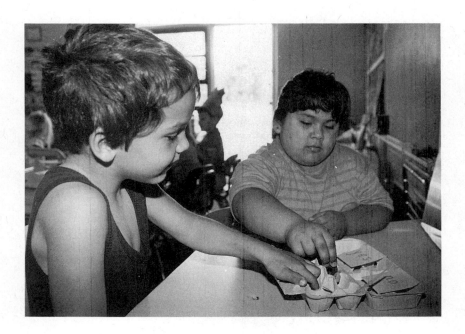

Science Concept

Magnets attract objects made of metal but not all metals.

Science Process Skill

To focus observations by using the senses.

Science Vocabulary

attract
magnet
magnetic
predict
sort

What to Do

1. Have children place one object into each compartment of the egg carton.

2. Will a magnet attract the objects? Ask the children to test each object with the magnet and to place it on the Yes or No side of the lid.

3. Encourage children to make guesses and to check each other's accuracy.

4. Have children work in pairs to fill an egg carton with new materials and ask their partner to predict which objects the magnet will attract. Have them empty their cartons and repeat the procedure with new objects.

Assessing the Activity

Select several objects that the class has been using during the activity. Ask the children to place each object on the Yes or No side and to check their predictions with a magnet.

ACTIVITY 2

Can You Stop a Magnet?

Materials (per group)

magnet
cardboard square (about 10 cm
× 10 cm)
paper clips
a variety of materials (about 10 cm
× 10 cm), such as aluminum, plastic,
rubber, wool, fabric, and duct tape
Discovery Journals

Magnetic force will pass through most objects. This property allows us to coat magnets with rubber, plastic, wood, or other materials and still preserve their strength and usefulness. Children will see in this activity how well a magnet will do its work through other materials.

Before the Activity

Prepare four to eight squares of materials per group (a variety is essential). Metal can be obtained from aluminum cans, but the owner of a heating and air conditioning business will have scrap iron and steel or aluminum pieces that he or she will be more than happy to cut for you. For safety, tape around the edges of the metal squares.

What to Do

1. The children know that magnets attract paper clips. Show them that a magnet will attract paper clips through the cardboard square.

C ▪ O ▪ N ▪ N ▪ E ▪ C ▪ T ▪ I ▪ O ▪ N ▪ S

To Language

Expressive Language - Children will talk about what they are discovering. Encourage them to use science words by using them yourself.

To Math

Comparing - Children will compare the ability of magnetic force to pass through various materials.

Counting - Children might count the number of objects that a magnet attracts through the various materials.

Science Concept

Magnetic force can pass through various materials.

Science Process Skill

To focus observations by using the senses.

Science Vocabulary

attract
compare
magnet
strength

2. Direct the children to place one or more of the other squares of cardboard on the first and see whether the magnet still attracts the paper clips. You might have the children count the number of paper clips picked up.

3. Encourage the children to experiment with different substances and thicknesses to see whether the various materials affect the number of paper clips the magnet will attract.

4. Discuss these experiences with the children to help them focus on possible conclusions and Discovery Journal entries.

5. Send home Magnet Family Connection Activity 1 (page 285).

Assessing the Activity

Listen to the children discuss the results of their explorations. Do their comments suggest an understanding of magnetic force passing through objects?

ACTIVITY 3

Up from the Sand

Materials

1 strong magnet (per group)

several other magnets

several objects that are attracted to a magnet, such as washers, bolts, nuts, and paper clips

box of sand or a water table filled with sand

Magnetic force travels through most materials—even materials we cannot see through, such as sand. Magnets can be tools of exploration, allowing us to locate objects that otherwise might not be discovered. This activity is similar to remote sensing exploration used to locate mineral resources below ground.

Before the Activity

Setting the stage for this activity is best done without the children present. Hide several of the objects just below the surface of the sand.

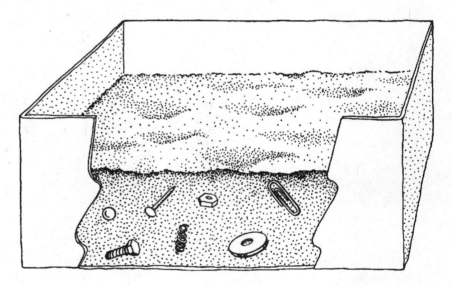

C▪O▪N▪N▪E▪C▪T▪I▪O▪N▪S

To Language

Expressive Language - Children will practice the new science vocabulary, particularly the word *attract*, as they work together.

Science Concept

Magnetic force can pass through various materials.

Science Process Skill

To focus observations by using the senses.

Science Vocabulary

attract
locate
magnetic
surface

What to Do

1. Ask a child to take a strong magnet and to move it slowly back and forth over the surface of the sand. The child should be in for a real surprise when objects come jumping out of the sand.

2. Now allow the children to work on their own, or in groups of two or four, to hide objects in the sand and then to locate them. Ask: What happens when you use different magnets?

3. A great field trip idea is to invite and watch a classroom visitor use a portable metal detector to locate coins and other objects in the school yard.

Assessing the Activity

Observe the children as they work. Do they try varying the depth of the objects? Do they try different magnets? Are focused observations apparent?

CHECKPOINT

What Is in the Box?

Materials

several covered boxes

steel washers

pennies

magnets

assorted objects, some attracted to a magnet and some not

Discovery Journals

This activity asks children to make observations and to extend those observations on the basis of the experiences they have had. The children should already know which objects are attracted to a magnet. Now they will apply this information to a set of unknown objects whose invisible reaction should trigger knowledge about attraction of magnets to certain materials.

Before the Activity

You will need several easily opened boxes, such as small jewelry boxes. Group the assorted objects in sets by difficulty. For example, Set 1 may have two easily recognized attracted/nonattracted pairs such as washers and buttons; Set 2, washers and pennies; and so on. Include ten multiple sets using brass, aluminum, iron, steel, and plastic.

What to Do

I. Say: Predict whether a magnet will attract a penny. Will it attract a washer? Have children explain their reasons for their predictions.

C･O･N･N･E･C･T･I･O･N･S

To Language

Expressive Language - Children will use the science vocabulary as they work in pairs. (As you talk with the children, encourage them to recall information from their previous experiences with magnets.)

Discovery Journals - Children will draw objects attracted by a magnet. (Suggest that children write captions, a way they can use their emerging literacy skills at their own level.)

Science Concept

Magnets attract objects made of metal but not all metals.

Science Process Skill

To focus observations by using the senses.

Science Vocabulary

attract

magnet

magnetism

predict

2. Have children work in pairs to place a washer or penny into a box and close the lid. Tell one child not to allow the other child to see the object.

3. Tell the second child to use the magnet to observe how the object in the box behaves and to state whether the object is a washer or a penny. Have the children explain why they made their choice.

4. Encourage the children to make their own "puzzlers" with other objects. Start them with buttons and metal and plastic paper clips.

5. Ask the children to draw or trace in their Discovery Journals several objects that they found to be attracted to a magnet.

Assessing the Activity

Individual demonstrations of accurate answers should be used to determine whether children are making careful observations. Your discussion with each child can determine the extent to which his or her previous observations have provided a basis on which to make accurate predictions.

ACTIVITY 4

Catch a Clip

Materials

2 rubber bands
large container with paper clips
2 bar magnets
string
2 fishing poles (optional)
Discovery Journals

The concept of *polarity* is essential to a continued exploration of magnetism, in this unit and later on in science. Magnets two have poles, a north and a south. The poles behave as if they were centers of force.

Before the Activity

Prepare each bar magnet by placing a rubber band tightly around the exact center. Hook a paper clip through the rubber band. Tie a long piece of string to the rubber band. Attach the string to a fishing pole if you like. Spread the paper clips evenly over the bottom of the container. Remind children that bar magnets lose their force when dropped or struck.

What to Do

1. Ask a child to lower a bar magnet into the container of paper clips and to withdraw it after it contacts the paper clips. Ask the children to observe where the paper clips stick to the magnet.

C ▪ O ▪ N ▪ N ▪ E ▪ C ▪ T ▪ I ▪ O ▪ N ▪ S

To Language

Expressive Language - Focus on comparative language, such as *strongest* and *weaker*.

Discovery Journals - Because the results are so visual, children will make drawings that clearly show the outcome of this activity.

To Math

Counting - Children will count the number of objects caught at each pole.

Comparing - Children will compare the number of objects caught at the north pole, south pole, and middle of the magnet.

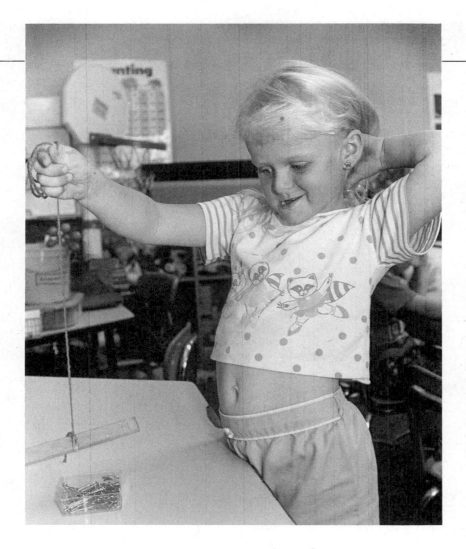

Science Concept

The strength of magnetic force varies.

Science Process Skill

To focus observations by using the senses.

Science Vocabulary

attract
bar magnets
compare

2. Remove the paper clips from both attracting ends of the magnet. Ask the child to repeat step 1 to see whether the same thing happens.

3. Invite the child to pick up the paper clips with different parts of the magnet. Ask: What parts of the magnet seem to be the strongest? Place the materials in the Discovery Center for all the children to use.

4. Have the children draw in their Discovery Journals what they observed in this activity.

Assessing the Activity

Children's Discovery Journal entries should indicate their understanding of the variation of magnetic strength found in different regions of a magnet.

ACTIVITY 5

Pulling Force

Materials

magnets of different sizes and strengths (1 per child)
paper clips
washers
Discovery Journals

Magnets have different strengths. This activity lets the children measure the relative strengths of magnets by determining how many paper clips the magnets can pull across a table.

Before the Activity

Prepare a number of paper clip chains of different lengths. Color code the magnets by putting a different colored sticker on each.

What to Do

1. Have the children prepare a tally sheet in their Discovery Journals. Alternatively, you may want to prepare tally charts for use with washers.

2. Ask each child to place a magnet at one end of a paper clip chain and to pull up slowly. Ask: Does the magnet pull the chain? (If it does not, have them try a shorter chain.) Ask: What is the longest chain the magnet can pull?

C▪O▪N▪N▪E▪C▪T▪I▪O▪N▪S

To Language

Expressive Language - Children will continue to practice comparative language (as they talk about the different magnets).

Discovery Journals - Children will learn a new way to record information: a tally sheet.

To Math

Counting - Children will count the number of paper clips each magnet can pull.

Comparing - Children will compare the magnets with each other according to their strength.

Science Concept

The strength of magnetic force varies.

Science Process Skill

To focus observations by using the senses.

Science Vocabulary

heavy
light
power
strength
strong
weak

3. When the children have found the longest chain their magnets can pull, invite them to make a mark on their tally sheets for each clip in the chain.

4. Have them repeat the process using a different magnet.

5. Ask: Which magnet is the strongest? Which magnet is the weakest? Are any equal in strength?

Assessing the Activity

Ask children to compare the strengths of the different magnets. Do they use the tally sheet successfully?

How strong is your magnet?

ACTIVITY 6

Magnetic Picker-Upper

Materials

2 donut magnets

small paper bag

several nonmetallic objects of the same type (e.g., plastic measuring cubes)

This activity allows children yet another opportunity to explore differences in the strengths of magnets and at the same time reinforce counting skills.

What to Do

1. Show the children how to pick up an empty paper bag by placing a magnet inside the bag while holding another magnet against the bag on the outside.

2. Have the children add one, two, three, and more objects to the bag and observe how many objects the magnet-bag-magnet system can hold before the bag and its contents fall.

3. Pass the bag around the room and let each child add objects to it. Have the group count in unison as each object is added to the bag.

4. Ask the children to try different magnet combinations, each time encouraging them to compare the number of counters that are held up by the different combinations.

5. Place the magnet-bag-magnet system in the Discovery Center. Let children continue to work independently to see how many objects they can hold in their own magnet-bag-magnet systems.

C·O·N·N·E·C·T·I·O·N·S

To Language

Expressive Language - Children will learn the word *compare*.

To Math

Counting - Children will count the objects put into a bag.

Comparing - Children will compare the number of objects each of the magnet-bag-magnet systems held.

Science Concept

The strength of magnetic force varies.

Science Process Skill

To focus observations by using the senses.

Science Vocabulary

compare

Assessing the Activity

Observe comparing and counting accuracy during the whole-group activity. Observe magnet-bag-magnet systems that children create at the Discovery Center.

ACTIVITY 7

Which Is the Strongest?

Materials

assortment of magnets of different sizes and types, such as bar and horseshoe magnets

double-pan balance

colored stickers

a collection of several iron and steel objects of different sizes and masses, such as paper clips and washers

Magnets have different strengths. This activity lets the children measure the relative strengths of magnets by determining which objects they can lift and which they cannot.

Before the Activity

If children do not know how to use the balance, provide them with an opportunity to become familiar with its use.

C ▪ O ▪ N ▪ N ▪ E ▪ C ▪ T ▪ I ▪ O ▪ N ▪ S

To Language

Expressive Language - Children will use expressive language. (This activity will give you the opportunity to assess the children's facility with the expressive language they have been using.)

To Math

Counting - Children will compare magnets according to strength.

Science Concept

The strength of magnetic force varies.

Science Process Skill

To focus observations by using the senses.

Science Vocabulary

compare
heavy
lift
light
strong
weak

What to Do

1. Have the children use the balance to determine which object from the collection is the heaviest and which is the lightest.

2. Ask them to select one magnet and try to pick up different objects with it.

3. Ask: What is the heaviest object this magnet can lift? Have the children put identical colored stickers on the magnet and on the heaviest object it can lift to identify the pair.

4. Have them follow the same procedure for the other magnets.

5. Ask: Which magnet is the strongest? Which magnet is the weakest?

Assessing the Activity

Ask the children to compare the strength of the magnets to determine if they understand the difference in strengths.

CHECKPOINT

Strong and Weak

Materials

variety of magnets of different sizes and strengths

magnetic game markers (Bingo markers)

sheets of paper with two concentric circles (20 cm and 15 cm in diameter) drawn on them

Discovery Journals

Some magnets are stronger than others. This activity lets the children compare the strength of magnets. They determine how strong each magnet is by discovering what it can pull out of a circle.

What to Do

1. Have the children, in pairs, put game markers inside the smaller circle.

2. Tell the children to run a magnet around the perimeter of the larger circle.

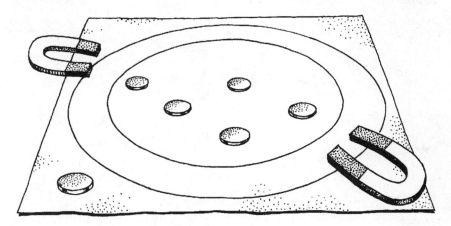

C▪O▪N▪N▪E▪C▪T▪I▪O▪N▪S

To Language

Discovery Journals - Children will record their findings.

To Math

Counting and Comparing - Children will count the number of game markers attracted by each magnet and use the information to compare the strength of the magnets.

Science Concept

The strength of magnetic force varies.

Science Process Skill

To focus observations by using the senses.

Science Vocabulary

strong
weak

3. Urge them to try the activity with other magnets and to find out which magnet is strongest by counting the number of markers that are pulled out of the circle by each magnet. Have them draw or write their results in their Discovery Journals.

4. Discuss which magnet the children found to be the strongest and which they found to be the weakest. Ask: Were any the same? Did everyone get the same results?

Assessing the Activity

Observe and discuss the findings. Do they accurately compare the strength of the magnets?

ACTIVITY 8

Bouncing Magnets

Materials (per child)

2 painted donut magnets
modeling clay
Discovery Journals
straw, or unsharpened pencil or
wooden dowel

Children explored the various aspects of magnetism during Free Discovery. Now they will focus on two important concepts of magnetism: *attraction* and *repulsion*. The predictability of these phenomena and their broader application to other science concepts that students will meet later are of great importance. To return again and again to the Discovery Center and find that magnets always work in the same, predictable way is essential for the young scientist.

Before the Activity

An easy way to prepare a bouncing magnet stand is to place a clay ball on the Discovery Center table and force an unsharpened pencil or dowel rod into the clay. This structure will allow the children to have their hands free to move the magnets.

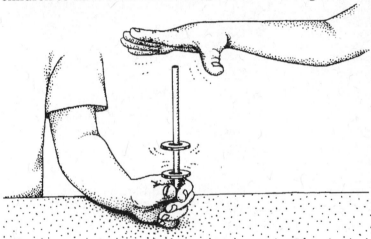

C ▪ O ▪ N ▪ N ▪ E ▪ C ▪ T ▪ I ▪ O ▪ N ▪ S

To Language

Expressive Language - You will be introducing new science vocabulary. Model its use often.

Discovery Journals - This activity is easy for the children to draw. Urge them to caption the drawings at their own skill level.

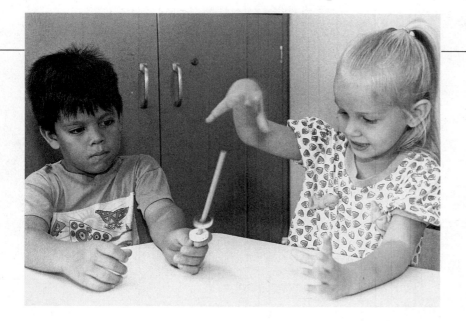

Science Concept

Magnets have poles; like poles repel and unlike poles attract.

Science Process Skill

To focus observations by using the senses.

Science Vocabulary

attract
predict
repel

What to Do

1. Request that the children hold one end of the pencil and slide one magnet over the other end. Ask them to slide a second magnet onto the pencil. If the two magnets attract each other, have the children take the magnet off, turn it over, and replace it. This time the magnets should repel each other and bounce on the pencil like a spring. Direct the children to add several other magnets so that they all bounce on the pencil. Encourage the children to push down on the top magnet and to feel the upward force.

2. Invite the children to predict whether two magnets will attract or repel each other. Be sure to have children explain why they made their predictions. When the children are able to predict successfully what a magnet arrangement will produce, distribute extra magnets. The children can make a stack of suspended bouncing magnets the height of the pencil.

3. Have children document their experiences in their Discovery Journals.

4. Send home Magnet Family Connection Activity 2 (page 285).

Assessing the Activity

Observe the children as they arrange the magnets to attract or repel other magnets. Do their placements of the magnets demonstrate an understanding of attraction and repulsion? Ask the child: Did you arrange the magnets to attract or repel?

ACTIVITY 9

What's the Big Attraction?

Materials

25 donut magnets (unpainted)

magnet board (see page 22)

Bouncing Magnets explored the most interesting aspect of magnetism. The fact that iron-containing material can be made to attract and repel has fascinated scientists for centuries. In this activity the children will discover the predictability of magnetic attraction and repulsion.

What to Do

1. Magnets and the magnet board can be left in the Discovery Center so that the children can explore the force of attraction and repulsion. You might challenge children to fit all the magnets on the magnet boards at once. Eventually children will observe that opposite sides of the magnets must be placed together (so that they attract) to fit the magnets on the wooden pegs.

2. Place two magnets on the board, with the opposite poles facing each other. Ask the children to tell you what they observe. Repeat the same process with two magnets with like poles placed together.

3. Have the children repeat the same process with like and opposite sides of the magnet and then tell you what they felt.

4. Encourage the children to continue to experiment with the equipment, creating patterns and games.

C▪O▪N▪N▪E▪C▪T▪I▪O▪N▪S

To Language

Expressive Language - Children will continue to practice new science vocabulary.

Science Concept

Magnets have poles; like poles repel and unlike poles attract.

Science Process Skill

To focus observations by using the senses.

Science Vocabulary

attract
force
magnet
repel

Assessing the Activity

Ask children to put two magnets on the board so that the magnets attract each other. Then ask them to place two magnets on the board so that they repel each other. If the children can accomplish these tasks at your request, they have observed that magnets have two different regions.

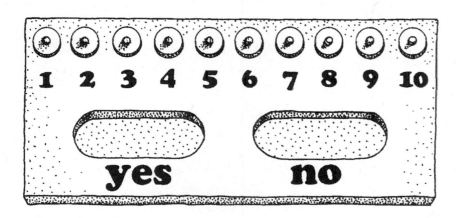

CHECKPOINT

Magnet Tag

Materials

1 unmarked donut magnet

By now the children have learned some things about polarity. This fun game will allow them to make use of their understanding of the concept.

What to Do

1. Have the children sit in a circle.

2. Demonstrate how to start the game by being "it" and moving around the circle. Move in front of a child and ask him or her to hold out the magnet so you can make one try at picking it up by touching it with one side of your magnet. It is important that the child hold the magnet securely enough to prevent it from flipping over.

3. If you are successful at capturing the child's magnet, then that child becomes "it." That child must take his or her magnet and try to capture another child's magnet. If the attempt is unsuccessful, the child must move around the circle until he or she captures another child's magnet.

C▪O▪N▪N▪E▪C▪T▪I▪O▪N▪S

To Language

Expressive Language - Children will continue to practice science vocabulary.

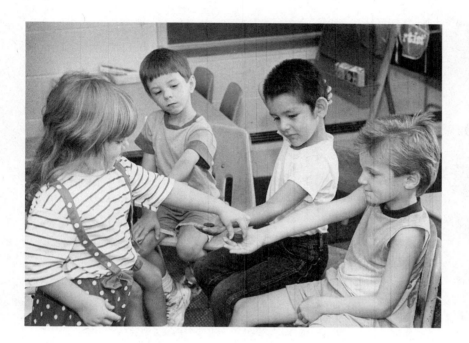

Science Concept

Magnets have poles; like poles repel and unlike poles attract.

Science Process Skill

To focus observations by using the senses.

Science Vocabulary

attract
repel

4. Continue the game until all children have had a turn at being "it."

5. Separate the class into smaller groups to speed up the pace of the game.

Assessing the Activity

Exchange marked magnets for unmarked ones. If children understand how *attract* and *repel* relate to polarity, they should be able to plan a capture by observing which pole the players have turned up in their hands.

ADDITIONAL STIMULATION

The Magnet Board Game

Materials

magnet board
20 unmarked magnets

The Magnet Board game uses the skills and knowledge gained from previous activities. Children who have mastered the concept of magnetism will use this knowledge to capture their magnets. For those who are developing their magnet knowledge, this game reinforces the predictability of the magnetic reactions.

What to Do

Show the children how to play the game. Play it with one of the children and let the others watch. Once you are satisfied with the instruction, place the magnet board in the Discovery Center.

How to play the Magnet Board game:

1. The first player separates and lays all twenty magnets on the table. The second player picks any ten magnets and puts one on each peg of the magnet board.

2. The first player chooses a magnet from those remaining on the table and attempts to pick up one of the magnets from the board. If the player is successful, the magnet is "captured" and the player places both magnets in that player's storage area. If the magnets are repelled, no magnet is captured and the player keeps the "test magnet." Whether the magnets are attracted or repelled, the player's turn is over.

3. The second player now chooses a magnet from the table and attempts to capture a magnet from the board.

4. Play continues until all the magnets are captured. The player with the tallest stack at the end of the game lays out the magnets for the next round.

C∙O∙N∙N∙E∙C∙T∙I∙O∙N∙S

To Math

Counting - Children will count the number of magnets captured by each player.

Science Concept

Magnets have poles; like poles repel and unlike poles attract.

Science Process Skill

To focus observations by using the senses.

Science Vocabulary

attract
capture
repel

Assessing the Activity

As the children become more experienced with the game, you will observe them recognizing the importance of turning over some of the magnets during the setup. They also will realize that they can get a "miss" on a second try if they turn their magnet over. Watch as they develop ways to make the game trickier for their opponents.

ACTIVITY 1

Stick or Slide?

Materials

magnet-strip chart

small bags

assorted objects, some attracted to a magnet and some not

The magnet-strip chart is a self-checking tool that allows the children to determine the magnetic nature of objects. If they have observed whether a magnet will attract particular objects, they should be able to make the choices provided by the strip board.

Before the Activity

Prepare the magnet-strip chart by gluing two strip magnets on a piece of cardboard or stiff tag board. Label the magnetic strips, one Yes and the other No. Place assorted objects into individual bags, varying the contents of the bags.

What to Do

1. Show the children how the magnet-strip chart works by putting several objects on the magnet strips according to whether the children believe they will be attracted.

2. To determine whether predictions are right or wrong, tilt the chart.

3. After the children have had some experience with this, have them work in pairs and predict whether objects will stick to the magnetic strips.

C▪O▪N▪N▪E▪C▪T▪I▪O▪N▪S

To Language

Expressive Language - Children will practice the science vocabulary as they work together to classify the objects.

To Math

Sorting and Classifying - Children will sort objects according to predictions of whether they will or will not be attracted to the magnet strip and classify the objects according to magnetic attraction.

Science Concept

Magnets attract objects made of metal but not all metals.

Science Process Skill

To use observations to classify.

Assessing the Activity

Observe the children's predictions and their verification of their predictions to determine whether they understand the magnetic attraction of different objects.

Science Vocabulary

attract
predict
test
magnetic

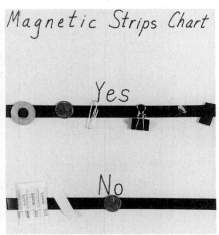

ACTIVITY 2

Magnets North and South

Materials

magnet board

several magnets with marked N and S poles (the test magnets)

several donut magnets without designated poles

This classification activity asks the children to sort a set of magnets by their poles. Although the activity appears simple, the concept is basic to an understanding of magnets. It causes children to focus on polarity and asks them to distinguish poles and to test that discrimination. If their classification skills are good, they should be able to create a whole line of magnets with the north poles facing up.

What to Do

1. Give the children the marked and unmarked magnets and the magnet board.

2. Explain that they are to sort the magnets by poles by placing one of the two poles face up. Demonstrate this with several magnets.

3. Show them how the test works by passing a test magnet over the magnet board. The test magnet should repel the sorted magnets. Incorrectly placed magnets will be attracted to the test magnet rather than repelled by it. Two children can work together, testing each other's work.

4. One extension and much more difficult sorting exercise would be to classify horseshoe, bar, and other magnets. Another extension would be for you to place the magnets on the board in a pattern (such as NSN or NNSS) and ask the children to continue the pattern.

C·O·N·N·E·C·T·I·O·N·S

To Math

Sorting - Children will sort objects according to polarity.

Patterning - Children might place unmarked magnets on the magnet board by following a pattern.

Science Concept

Magnets have poles; like poles repel and unlike poles attract.

Science Process Skill

To use observations to classify.

Science Vocabulary

attract
pattern
pole
repel
sort

Assessing the Activity

The children should be able to tell how the magnets are organized and to test for polarity. Have the children place all of their magnets, north side up, on the magnet board. You can quickly check the magnetic classification by bringing the north pole of a magnet close. If the children are correct, the magnets should not be attracted.

CHECKPOINT

Yes or No: The Magnet Knows

Materials

2 containers (of equal size and large enough to hold the objects in the bag) marked Yes and No

Discovery Journals

bags of assorted objects, such as pennies, nails, steel and aluminum paper clips, buttons, iron washers, soda can tabs, and fasteners (such as nuts, screws, and brass nails)

Classifying objects requires separating them into groups by known characteristics. In this activity, objects will be separated according to whether or not they are attracted to magnets. Recording the data allows them to check their skills as they move to a new bag of materials.

Before the Activity

Prepare the collections and number each bag.

What to Do

1. Have the children classify into the container marked Yes the objects that they predict the magnet will attract. Request that they count the number of objects in the Yes container and record this number in their Discovery Journals.

2. Tell them to place the remaining objects in the container marked No and then to count and record this number.

C ▪ O ▪ N ▪ N ▪ E ▪ C ▪ T ▪ I ▪ O ▪ N ▪ S

To Language

Discovery Journals - Children will draw and caption entries.

To Math

Sorting, Classifying, and Counting - Children will sort objects according to their predictions of magnetic attraction, classify the objects according to the reaction to magnetic force, and count the number of objects they predict will be attracted or not attracted to the magnet.

Science Concept

Magnets attract objects made of metal but not all metals.

Science Process Skill

To use observations to classify.

Science Vocabulary

attract
classify
group
magnetic
nonmagnetic
predict
sort

3. Now have them check their classification of the objects by using their magnets. Explain that they should touch the magnet to each object in the Yes container. Ask: Are all the objects pulled to the magnet? Direct children to place those that are not into the container marked No.

4. Next tell them to touch their magnet to the objects in the No container. Ask: Are any objects attracted to the magnet? If so, place them in the Yes container.

5. Ask: How are the objects that were attracted to the magnet alike?

6. Have the children draw a picture in their Discovery Journals of an object that surprised them. Was it a Yes or a No item?

7. Have the children empty the containers, and try the process again until all bags have been used.

8. Send home Magnet Family Connection Activity 3 (page 285).

Assessing the Activity

Observe the accuracy of the children as they sort the objects.

ADDITIONAL STIMULATION

Refrigerator Fun

Materials

paper
magnets

Most homes have a resource for teaching classification skills using magnets: the refrigerator. Children enjoy taking their daily creations home and hanging them on the refrigerator with household magnets. This activity brings magnetism into the child's world in a hands-on way that they will remember.

Before the Activity

Send home Magnet Family Connection Activity 4 (page 285). The activity lets families try this activity in their homes with their child and asks them to encourage their child to discuss observations with them. Send home magnets if necessary.

C•O•N•N•E•C•T•I•O•N•S

To Language

Espressive Language - Children will share their school experience with their families. (Family interest will reinforce school learning.)

To Math

Counting - Children will count the number of papers that their home magnets will hold.

Science Concept

The strength of magnetic force varies.

Science Process Skills

To use observations to classify.

Science Vocabulary

compare
strength

What to Do

1. Challenge the children to hang papers on the refrigerator
    using magnets. Have them use standard notebook paper. You
    may want to send some children's artwork home on the right
    sized paper to get them started.

2. Ask: Can one magnet hold up one sheet of paper? Two? Tell
    the class to continue adding sheets of paper until the magnet
    will no longer hold them up.

3. Have the children experiment with other magnets. They may
    want to bring their strongest magnet to school. Can they
    group magnets according to strength? Can they find other
    ways to classify the magnets?

Assessing the Activity

Children can discuss with you the strength of home magnets.
"Mine could hold one." "I've got one that will hold five pieces at
the same time!"

ACTIVITY 1

How Strong Is Your Magnet?

Materials (per pair)

2 magnets of obvious difference in magnetic strength

assorted other magnets

Discovery Journals

small container with several paper clips or small washers

Magnets come in a variety of shapes and strengths. The strongest magnets are electromagnets and are found in shipyards and scrap yards where they move tons of metal. Magnets can be classified by their strength. Children will use the number of objects that can be attracted and held by a magnet to compare strength. This is a data-gathering activity that will require the children to complete a chart of the number of washers or clips picked up by each magnet.

What to Do

1. Ask the children, in pairs, to lower the first magnet into the container of washers or paper clips and to withdraw the magnet upon contact with washers or clips.

2. Have the children count and record on a data table in their Discovery Journals the number of washers or clips that the magnet lifts from the box. To make a data table, they draw the magnet, then draw next to it the number of items that the magnet attracted.

3. Ask them to repeat the process with the second magnet.

4. Invite them to compare the magnets. Ask: Which lifted the most washers or clips? Why?

C ▪ O ▪ N ▪ N ▪ E ▪ C ▪ T ▪ I ▪ O ▪ N ▪ S

To Language

Espressive Language - Children will review the use of comparative terms.

Discovery Journals - Children will communicate findings by completing a data table.

To Math

Comparing and Place Value - Children will count the number of objects that each magnet attracts and record the information in their Discovery Journals.

Comparing - Children will compare magnets according to strength.

Science Concept

The strength of magnetic force varies.

Science Process Skill

To organize and communicate observations.

Science Vocabulary

compare
strength

5. Have children repeat the process with a third magnet and compare the strength of this magnet with the other two magnets. Tell them to record this information on the data table. Encourage them to try other magnets in the Discovery Center. Ask: Which is the strongest magnet?

6. As a good summary group activity, compare individual findings.

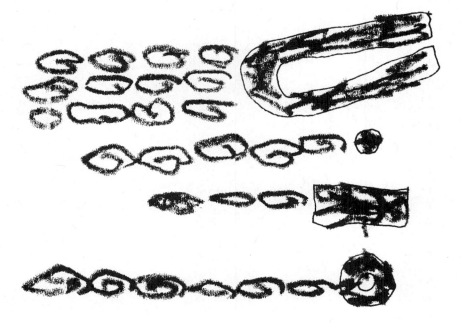

Assessing the Activity

Do the data tables in the Discovery Journals indicate an understanding of how charts are used to communicate information?

ACTIVITY 2

Wet Magnets

Materials (per pair or group)

assorted objects that can be placed in water, some attracted to a magnet and some not

2 water-filled containers marked Yes and No

magnet fastened to a string or fishing pole

Discovery Journals

Once the phenomenon of magnetic attraction with magnets has been mastered, the children are ready for new explorations. A more sophisticated concept is that magnetic attraction or repulsion is present in other mediums and through other materials. In this case the children will see that magnets act the same in water as they do in air. The rules hold the same for most liquids. For this activity water will work just fine.

Before the Activity

Prepare the two containers of water and the collection of objects. The string on the magnet will be adequate, but a fishing pole adds a bit of fun. One child can fish, and the other can watch the magnet work.

C ▪ O ▪ N ▪ N ▪ E ▪ C ▪ T ▪ I ▪ O ▪ N ▪ S

To Language

Discovery Journals - Children will draw a picture to communicate the results.

To Math

Sorting and Classifying - Children will sort objects according to predictions and classify objects according to how they responded to the magnet under water.

Science Concept

Magnetic force can pass through various materials.

Science Process Skill

To organize and communicate observations.

Science Vocabulary

attract
magnetic
nonmagnetic

What to Do

1. Have the children work in pairs and drop the objects into the water-filled Yes and No containers according to their guess as to whether the objects will be attracted to a magnet while under water.

2. Ask the children to lower the magnet into the containers to observe whether they attract objects under water.

3. Invite the children to share their results by drawing pictures in their Discovery Journals of what happened to the objects in each container.

4. Discuss this experience with the children. Ask: Does water change the way a magnet works?

Assessing the Activity

Do the children's drawings communicate the effect of water on magnetic force?

ACTIVITY 3

Magnetic Seek and Find

Materials

variety of magnets

small objects attracted to a magnet, such as washers and paper clips

2 identical maps of the classroom

objects for map markers, such as small blocks or rocks

This activity encourages children to use their cognitive abilities to locate magnets and objects that they cannot actually see, as they did in Focusing Observations Activity 3, Up from the Sand (see page 32). You will ask them to communicate what they have found in chart form.

Before the Activity

Maps can be as simple or sophisticated as those shown here. You might want to laminate them.

What to Do

1. Begin this activity by placing one map on the table. Ask one child to slide several objects that are attracted to magnets under the map in various locations.

2. Give the second map and a map marker to a child who has not observed where the objects were placed. Have this child use a magnet to try to locate an object under the map.

3. Explain that each time an object is located under the map, the child is to mark its location on the second map.

4. Encourage the children to work in pairs, taking turns hiding the objects under the map and finding the objects and marking their locations.

C▪O▪N▪N▪E▪C▪T▪I▪O▪N▪S

To Language

Expressive Language - This is a good time to reinforce accurate use of location words.

To Math

Mapping - Children will make connections between maps and actual locations in the room.

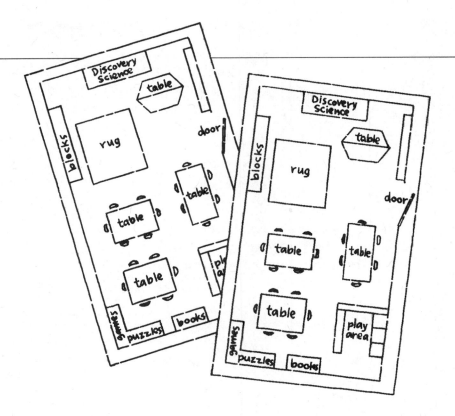

Science Concept

Magnetic force can travel through various materials.

Science Process Skill

To organize and communicate observations.

Science Vocabulary

attract
location
magnetic
map

Assessing the Activity

Observe the children as they search for, locate, and mark the locations of the hidden objects. Can the children describe the location of the hidden objects and place a marker in its actual classroom location?

CHECKPOINT

The Great Attraction Hunt

Materials (per child)

magnet sticker (self-adhesive note)
magnet
Discovery Journals

This Checkpoint is one way to determine whether the children can distinguish common objects attracted to magnets. The attraction hunt appears to be a fast-moving game but really is testing skills of observation that have been established in the previous activities. Observation on your part will determine which children are having success in this hunt.

Before the Activity

Prepare the magnet stickers by drawing a big *M* for *magnet* on each self-adhesive note. You also may want to prepare the room for a more interesting hunt by bringing in a few additional or unusual magnetic or nonmagnetic objects. A brass lamp will prove to be nonmagnetic, while your chalkboard may attract a magnet.

What to Do

1. Distribute a magnet sticker to each child.

2. Say: Look around the room. What things, like furniture, windows, and books, do you see that you think will attract a magnet? Have the children place their stickers on what they think will attract a magnet. Some will place stickers on the same object.

C ▪ O ▪ N ▪ N ▪ E ▪ C ▪ T ▪ I ▪ O ▪ N ▪ S

To Language

Discovery Journals - Children will record their findings.

To Math

Classifying - Children will classify items found in the classroom according to response to a magnet.

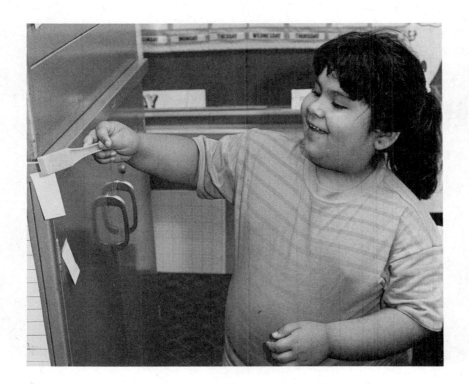

Science Concept

Magnets attract objects made of metal but not all metals.

Science Process Skill

To organize and communicate observations.

Science Vocabulary

attract
magnetic
nonmagnetic
predict
test

3. Now have them test the predictions. Give each child a magnet. Let them move about the room to check the accuracy of their predictions. As they test their predictions, have them record what they found out by drawing the place they chose in their Discovery Journals.

4. Have the children remove the stickers and repeat the activity, only now the rule is "only one sticker on any object."

5. Again have the children record in their Discovery Journals the location and what they found.

6. This activity may be repeated several times.

7. An extension would be to use the classroom map from the previous activity. Can the children mark locations on the classroom map where they found objects attracted by a magnet?

Assessing the Activity

Check accuracy of responses. It is important not to evaluate the children on the accuracy of the prediction but rather on their ability to make and record accurate observations.

ADDITIONAL STIMULATION

Fishing with Magnets

Materials (per group)

30 foam balls in 3 different colors

30 thumb tacks

magnet wands (bingo wands), or bar or other large magnets

large plastic container or cardboard box

1 timer

1-inch-square graph paper (per child)

pole and string, or fishing pole (optional)

crayons, in colors to match the foam balls

This activity provides a means for the children to organize and communicate information relative to their individual skill at putting the power of magnetism to work.

Before the Activity

Stick a thumb tack into each foam ball. Put the balls into the cardboard box. An interesting variation of this activity would be to use fishing poles: attach one end of a string to a pole and tie the other end of the string to a horseshoe magnet.

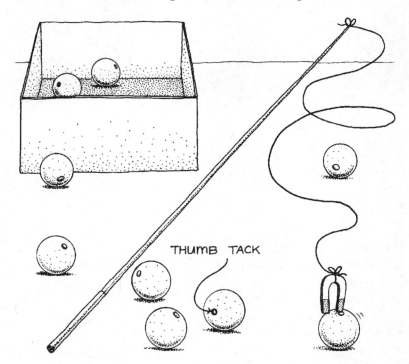

THUMB TACK

C▪O▪N▪N▪E▪C▪T▪I▪O▪N▪S

To Math

Counting and Graphing - Children will count and graph the number of colored balls picked up.

Science Concept

Magnets attract objects made of metal but not all metals.

Science Process Skill

To organize and communicate information.

Science Vocabulary

classify
count
graph
group
sort

What to Do

1. Place the cardboard box on the floor.

2. Instruct the children to lower the magnet wand into the box and to pick up as many balls as possible in 1 minute. Set the timer for each turn that is taken. Give each child one turn.

3. Tell each child to count the number of each color of ball that they picked up during their 1-minute attempt.

4. Show the children how to make a bar graph by coloring the same number of squares on the graph paper as the number of balls picked up in each color group.

Assessing the Activity

Can the children get information from a simple bar graph?

UNIT 2

Rocks and Soil

Essential Information

Rocks are solid pieces of the earth's crust, made up of one or more different minerals. Rocks are of three major types: igneous, sedimentary, and metamorphic. Igneous rocks are formed when magma solidifies; granite, pumice, and obsidian are good examples. Sedimentary rocks are the largest group and are formed by the cementing together of particles of rock, clay, or sand; shale, limestone, and sandstone are examples. Metamorphic rocks are the least common and are formed when igneous or sedimentary rocks are placed under extreme heat or pressure or when a chemical change takes place in their composition; slate, quartz, and marble are examples of metamorphic rocks.

Science Concepts

The following science concepts will be addressed in the Rocks and Soil unit:

1. Rocks have unique physical properties, and these properties can be used for classification.

2. Soils have unique physical properties, and soil is an important component of the natural world.

Getting Ready

Add the following materials to the Discovery Center:

- humus (peat, compost, or commercial potting soil)
- potting soil
- clay (powdered pottery clay)
- sand
- garden soil
- a large selection of rocks in many sizes, shapes, and colors
- newsprint
- toothpicks
- tools to shape clay, such as spoons, sticks, and forks
- masking tape (for labels)
- planting containers
- coffee cans with lids
- Cuisenaire® rods
- geodes

Minerals are naturally occurring elements or inorganic compounds. Between 2,000 and 2,500 different minerals are found in the earth's crust. Most of the rocks your children will bring in to class will be made up of only eight common minerals. The children may ask the names of the rocks they are working with. Naming rocks is not the focus of any activity in the Rocks and Soil unit, yet children often find the names interesting. Learn the names if you want to. It is nice to be able to share them with the children.

Some important rock and mineral characteristics:

- *Color.* Although often used to identify specimens, color may not always be an accurate property to use for identification.
- *Streak.* Minerals leave a characteristic streak when rubbed across unglazed porcelain, revealing the color of the powder of the mineral.
- *Hardness.* A measure of how easily a rock or mineral can be scratched.
- *Luster.* Characterized by the way light is reflected from the surface of the specimen (shiny to dull).
- *Crystal form or shape.* Used for identification.

Soil is a mixture of small clay, sand, and organic (decaying plant and animal material) particles. Different types of soils have characteristic amounts of these three materials. Because soils are different in their composition, they have different physical characteristics. For example, some soils retain large amounts of water, while others can barely hold any water at all.

Types of soil:

- *Organic* (humus). A mixture of decaying plant and animal remains, as in peat, compost, or commercial potting soil
- *Clay.* Small, tightly packed soil particles
- *Sand.* Large soil particles made up of silicon dioxide
- *Silt.* Extremely fine particles that have settled out of water
- *Loam.* Fertile, fine-textured particles that drain well
- *Loess.* Fine clay soil particles that were carried by the wind

You may want to send a letter to families to announce the Rocks and Soil unit (see the Family Connection, page 286, for an example). Explain that children may bring additional soil samples or rocks from home. Provide the children with small sampling containers, such as sandwich bags, to avoid unmanageable volumes of dirt. Label each sample with the name of the child who collected it and the place from where it came.

Soil samples may be collected from locations around the school, perhaps by the entire class as a research expedition. When scientists collect soil samples, they take several small samples from an area and mix them to get a representative sample. You can duplicate this process. In each area sampled, ask each child to collect a spoonful to place in the sample container. Label the samples with the locations.

Children may bring more soil samples or rocks from home. Provide them with small sampling containers such as plastic bags to avoid unmanageable volumes of dirt. Label all the samples with the name of the collector and the location in which they were found.

Materials

large sheet of newsprint (for a Discovery Chart)
markers
tape
rock and soil materials
Success in Science Inventory (see page 17)
Discovery Journals

Free Discovery

You may want to use the Success in Science Inventory and Discovery Journal entries to evaluate the children's progress during Free Discovery.

What to Do

1. Assemble the children in one area of the room. Work together to discuss and record all that they know about rocks and soil. Accept all the children's comments and write them on a Discovery Chart displayed in front of the group. If the children's comments are repeated, call attention to that fact. One approach might be: "Children, listen to your friends. Listen to what they are saying so that you can say something different."

   Begin the discussion with open-ended questions, avoiding questions with yes-or-no answers. A few questions might be: What do you know about rocks and soil? Where do you find rocks and soil? What happens when rocks and soil get wet? How can rocks and soil move? What do we use rocks and soil for?

What We Know About Rocks
We eat a rock. (salt rock)
Rocks are hard.
Some rocks have gold in them.
Rocks are different colors.
Some rocks are soft.
Some rocks can write.
Rocks are different sizes.
Sand is rock.
Some rocks break when dropped.
Some rocks are made into jewelry.

2. After accepting and recording all comments, review them. Tape the Discovery Chart to a wall.

3. Talk about the new materials in the Discovery Center. Be sure children understand the proper way to handle rocks and soil samples. After use, all rocks and soil should be cleaned up and saved for later discovery activities.

4. Begin Free Discovery. Have the children work at the Discovery Center to find out even more about rocks and soil. Allow children to explore freely the properties of the rocks and soil samples, mixing, adding water, looking at them with hand lenses, and so on. Encourage them to write and draw about their discoveries in their Discovery Journals. Later they will share their information in a large-group discussion, and it will be used to create more Discovery Charts.

5. Record individual performance using the Success in Science Inventory.

6. Reassemble the class into a large group. Restate the comments recorded on the Discovery Chart, and ask the children to share drawings and writings from their Discovery Journals. Add the new information to the Discovery Chart in a different color. Call the children's attention to the new discoveries they have made during their free exploration. Then ask: What else would you like to learn about rocks and soil?

STORY TIME

Use this story-telling activity, the Legend of the Geode (jē´ōd), to raise the children's interest in rocks and soil. If possible, show a geode, or a picture of a geode, to the children.

Legend of the Geode

Once upon a time in a village not very far from here there lived the happiest people in the whole world. They were so happy that as they went about their daily lives, they were constantly singing, whistling, humming, and talking with each other. No one *ever* got mean or angry. It was a *wonderful* village.

One fine spring day a giant came into the village, looking for a place to live. The people were so happy and friendly that they offered the giant a place to live. It wasn't long before the giant demanded that the people of the village plant his garden. He ordered them to hoe it and to pick its vegetables every day when it was very hot! Even though the villagers were confused by the giant's orders and how grouchy he was, they still sang and whistled and hummed and talked with each other as they worked.

After the vegetables were all picked, the grouchy giant ordered the people to clean his house. He made them scrub the walls and floors with toothbrushes! He made them shine the pots and pans with cotton balls! And he made them change the sheets on his giant bed ten times a day! The poor villagers were very tired and very confused, but still very happy. So, as they cleaned the giant's house every day, they would still sing and hum and whistle and talk with each other.

The giant hated all the noise their singing and humming and whistling and talking created, so he ordered them to HUSH! They couldn't hush; they didn't know how to not sing, hum, whistle, and talk. So they kept on making the noise that the giant hated. He again ordered them to HUSH! He told them that if they did not hush, he would cast a spell on them and take away their songs, hums, whistles, and voices! But they could not hush.

All of a sudden, the giant came into the house, carrying a round stone. He slowly moved it over the villagers' heads, and one by one their sounds disappeared. Try as they did, the people could not sing a note, or hum a tune, or whistle a sound, or say one little word. Tears began to stream down the faces of the once-happy villagers.

The giant was very satisfied with himself, and he decided to leave the village to go and be mean somewhere else. Before he left, he put the powerful stone in the middle of the village. As the people watched him leave, they gathered together to cry near the stone. A young girl, not much bigger than you, _____, went over to the stone. Suddenly she became very strong. The people formed a circle around her as she picked up the stone and broke it open. All at once the people said AH! OH! OOH! Their voices had been set free out of the beautiful geode! And once again you could hear them sing and hum and whistle and talk!

ACTIVITY 1

Not All Rocks Look Alike

Materials (per group of four)

4 rocks
4 hand lenses
paper bag
Discovery Journals

A rock pile from a distance may look like a collection of identical rocks, but every rock in the world is unique. This is an observation activity that will focus the children on visual observations of rock characteristics.

Before the Activity

Select the rocks for the activity depending on the experience and skill level of the group. You may want to repeat this activity several times. Begin with a collection of rocks that have obvious similarities and differences. As the children become more "rock conscious," give them increasingly similar rocks. Familiarize yourself with the characteristics of the rocks, such as color, shape, texture, and luster.

C ▪ O ▪ N ▪ N ▪ E ▪ C ▪ T ▪ I ▪ O ▪ N ▪ S

To Language

Expressive Language - Before the activity, children will use the science vocabulary to describe their rock. During the activity, they will use their vocabulary to compare their rock with the rocks of other children. (It will be interesting to listen to the words the children use in their descriptions.)

Discovery Journals - Children will draw pictures of their rocks. (An exciting addition would be to have the children dictate their own Legend of the Geode story, using their rock as the story focus.)

To Math

Comparing - Children might compare their rock with a partner's rock.

What to Do

1. This activity works best in groups of four. Ask each child to choose a rock and to describe the rock to the group.

2. Tell the children to draw their rocks in their Discovery Journals.

3. Alert them to look at their rocks very carefully for color, shape, and crystals.

4. Have the children put each of their rocks into the paper bag and gently shake the bag.

5. Invite one child in each group to dump the rocks out onto the table. Ask: Can you find your rock? How do you know this is your rock? Say: Tell someone in your group how you know this is your rock.

6. You might have children find a partner with a similar-size rock, a rock of the same color, or any other suitable attribute for comparison, and compare the two rocks.

7. Send home Rocks and Soil Family Connection Activity 1 (page 287).

Assessing the Activity

Describe the visual characteristics of a particular rock and ask the children to select the described rock from a group of rocks.

Science Concept

Rocks have unique physical properties, and these properties can be used for classification.

Science Process Skill

To focus observations by using the senses.

Science Vocabulary

compare

descriptive words such as dull, sparkly, shiny, and rough

magnify

observation

various attributes of color, shape, texture, crystals

ACTIVITY 2

Blind-Folded Rock Swap

Materials (per group)

rocks

paper bag

Children can begin to explore rock identification by using the sense of touch. Texture, layering, hardness, and shape all may be examined by touch. Touch is a good way to introduce children to the variety of rock characteristics.

Before the Activity

For this activity, select rocks that have an interesting feel to them; for example, heavy, light, rough, or slick. The children will need to be able to observe the differences readily. Some unique rocks you might try are pumice, granite with relatively large quartz crystals, obsidian (glassy lava rock), chalk, sandstone, and coal.

What to Do

1. Have the children work in pairs or groups of four. Direct them each to select a rock from the collection. Encourage them to talk about how their rocks feel. Ask: Is it your rock's texture, weight, size, shape, or something else that makes your rock feel different from other rocks?

2. Have the children place the rocks into their group's paper bag and gently mix them up.

C▪O▪N▪N▪E▪C▪T▪I▪O▪N▪S

To Language

Expressive Language - Some of the science vocabulary will be familiar to the children, as they probably have used the terms to describe other objects or events in their lives. However, terms such as *grainy, slick,* and *coarse* will most likely be new to them. Listen carefully for the children to use these new words and also to see whether they carry the words over into other areas of your curriculum.

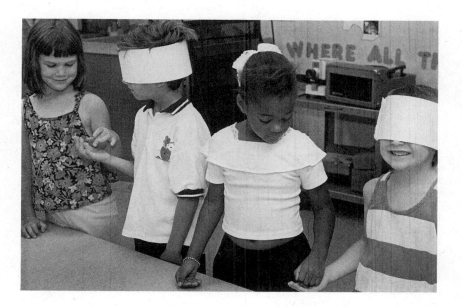

Science Concept

Rocks have unique physical properties, and these properties can be used for classification.

Science Process Skill

To focus observations by using the senses.

Science Vocabulary

coarse
grainy
hard
pointed
rough
sharp
slick
slippery
smooth
soft
texture

3. Have each group member, without looking in the bag, take turns handling the rocks and observing what they feel. Give each child the opportunity to try to identify his or her own rock, to remove it from the bag, and to keep it tightly covered in their hands.

4. When everyone is ready, tell them to open their hands. Ask: Do you have your own rock? How do you know this is your rock?

5. Repeat the activity, this time combining two or three groups. Can the children find their rock in this larger set?

Assessing the Activity

Using stickers, number the rocks that the children are using in this activity. Have each child record his or her rock's number before putting it into the bag. Observe whether the children can find their original rocks.

What Is That Rock's Mass?

ACTIVITY 3

Materials (per group)

double-pan balance
several rocks of differing masses
Discovery Journals
nonstandard masses, such as counting cubes, washers, small ceramic tiles, and animal counters

The balance is an important scientific tool, as mass and weight are critical observations in almost every scientific endeavor. The more experiences children have in this area, the better they will understand these concepts later. In this activity the children will add the idea of specific measurement units to their experience of light and heavy.

Before the Activity

This activity may be done as a whole class in the Discovery Center or with groups of two or four. Select rocks that are not so large that they take too many counters for the children to handle. To prepare for Assessing the Activity, determine the mass of each of the numbered specimens with the nonstandard units the children will be using. Record this information on a card to carry with you as you observe the children at work.

C▪O▪N▪N▪E▪C▪T▪I▪O▪N▪S

To Language

Discovery Journals - Children will record comparisons.

To Math

Measuring and Graphing - Children will estimate a rock's mass by comparing its mass to the mass of ordinary objects. Children might help you develop a class graph comparing rock masses.

Science Concept

Rocks have unique physical properties, and these properties can be used for classification.

Science Process Skill

To focus observations by using the senses.

Science Vocabulary

balance
heavier
lighter
mass
weight

What to Do

1. Provide the children with a variety of small rocks and non-standard masses. Encourage the children to choose one rock each and then to imagine something in their homes that is heavier (or lighter) than the particular rock.

2. Have them draw the object in their Discovery Journals and trace their rock next to the drawing.

3. Have the children find the mass of each rock in terms of a nonstandard mass by putting a rock on one side of the balance, putting nonstandard masses on the other side, and counting the number of nonstandard masses needed to level the balance. Have the children record the findings in their Discovery Journals.

4. You might have the children help you develop a class graph comparing the masses of individual rocks or team rocks. Use the actual rocks along one axis and the nonstandard units along the other.

5. Have the children repeat the activity using a different nonstandard mass.

Assessing the Activity

Ask the children to record or verbalize the masses of their rock specimens in nonstandard units. Compare their answers against the masses you previously determined for the rocks.

ACTIVITY 4

Greater Than, Less Than, or Equal?

Materials (per group)

rocks

double-pan balance

nonstandard masses such as counting cubes, washers, or animal counters

Discovery Journals

The emerging scientist must have many opportunities to determine quantitative values for objects, and a firm grounding in measurement provides a foundation for further exploration. Mass and linear measurement are fairly simple for young learners, whereas volume, area, density, temperature, and conductivity require more sophisticated equipment and skills. This activity provides yet another experience with the mass of rocks and the use of the balance.

Before the Activity

Encourage the children to bring in their own small rocks. Model the concepts of greater than, less than, or equal by comparing several rocks on the balance in front of them.

What to Do

1. Select a rock. With the children, determine the rock's mass using the nonstandard unit. Have the children record the measurement in their Discovery Journals.

2. Now tell them work independently or in pairs to select other rocks and determine whether they are greater than, less than, or equal in mass to the original.

C▪O▪N▪N▪E▪C▪T▪I▪O▪N▪S

To Language

Discovery Journals - Children will record measurements and comparisons.

To Math

Measuring and Comparing - As the children progress through this activity, they will enjoy testing whether they can find rocks with the same mass or with very different masses.

Mass

Science Concept

Rocks have unique physical properties, and these properties can be used for classification.

Science Process Skill

To focus observations by using the senses.

Science Vocabulary

different
equal
greater than
less than
same

3. Direct them to record the results of their measurements of two or three rocks in their Discovery Journals.

Assessing the Activity

Have the children observe as you place a rock on the balance pan and measure its mass using a nonstandard unit of measure. The children should be able to state the comparative mass of the rock by using the terms *greater than*, *less than*, and *equal to*.

CHECKPOINT

Do You See the Rock I See?

Materials

several rocks, with a variety of attributes

Children love chants and rhythms. This Checkpoint activity incorporates the fun of a chant with the children's awareness of the unique physical properties of rocks.

Before the Activity

Take time to assess the ability levels of the children and to determine how you want to divide the groups or if you want to involve the entire class.

What to Do

1. Spread out several rocks with different attributes in front of the children.

2. Say in a chanting manner: I see a rock, and it is (describe one of the rocks, using attributes the children have been observing). Tailor your descriptions to the levels of understanding of the individual children. Point to one of the children in the group as you ask: Do you know which rock I see?

C·O·N·N·E·C·T·I·O·N·S

To Language

Semantics - When children are able to identify the rocks described in the chant correctly, they have come to a level of understanding of those particular characteristics. When they can say the chant using the correct science vocabulary, they have developed greater expressive language skills. This is a very exciting development for a teacher to witness.

Science Concept

Rocks have unique physical properties, and these properties can be used for classification.

Science Process Skill

To focus observations by using the senses.

Science Vocabulary

rock attributes, such as shiny/dull, rough/smooth, big/small, long/round

3. This chant may be repeated for every child in the group. It also may be used among the children as an extension activity.

4. Send home Rocks and Soil Family Connection Activity 2 (page 287).

Assessing the Activity

This activity allows for the individual evaluation of how well each child is developing the skills of observation and the language associated with this unit. Is their vocabulary more varied than at the beginning of the unit? Are they noticing more details? Are their descriptions more accurate?

ADDITIONAL STIMULATION

Rock Hound Expedition

Materials

large variety of rocks
large bucket

Part of every geologist's work is field trips. Through field study new locations for mineral or ore deposits are found. Field trips can become real adventures. Keep this in mind as you place the rock treasures around the expedition site.

Before the Activity

Seed the school yard or other site with the rocks.

What to Do

1. Think about the children who need help with observation and expression as you form groups. Some children will benefit from being grouped with children who are strong models. Other children may be more expressive with an adult, such as a volunteer family member or a classroom aide, or a good friend.

C ▪ O ▪ N ▪ N ▪ E ▪ C ▪ T ▪ I ▪ O ▪ N ▪ S

To Language

Expressive Language - Children will share with each other the size, shape, color, and feel of their rocks. (Field trips are great stimulators for language interaction, particularly if the location is especially interesting or new to the children.)

To Math

Grouping and Counting - Children will group their rocks by special characteristics (size, shape, feel, weight, color) and count the number of rocks they have in each group, as well as the total number of rocks found.

Science Concept

Rocks have unique physical properties, and these properties can be used for classification.

Science Process Skill

To focus observations by using the senses.

Science Vocabulary

descriptive words of a rock's various attributes (size, shape, texture, weight, color, or other special characteristics)

rock names

2. Take the class on an expedition to gather the rocks and put them in the bucket. During the trip stimulate observations and descriptive language by questioning, comparing, and contrasting the various rocks they find. The more enthusiastic and encouraging you are, the more interested and excited the children will be.

3. When the children return to the classroom, ask them to group their rocks into the categories discussed in previous activities.

4. Challenge the children to count the number of rocks in each group, as well as the total number of rocks found.

5. Have the children play Do You Have a Rock Like Mine? Each child chooses a rock. One person holds up a rock. Everyone checks his or her rock to see if it is the same type. Then you ask for words to describe what is special about the rock, such as shiny, dull, heavy, and smooth.

6. After this activity, you may want to have the children design displays for a rock show or create their own rock museum.

Assessing the Activity

Throughout this field experience, interact with the children and assess their skills at observation and expression. Do they notice details? Do they realize that one rock can be described in many different ways?

ACTIVITY 5

Smells of the Earth

Materials

1 large container each of clay, sand, potting soil, and playground soil

spoons (1 or 2 per group)

small cups (8 per group)

droppers (1 or 2 per group)

trays, such as plastic foam deli trays (1 or 2 per group)

newsprint

crayons

The smell of fresh earth and rain trigger memories in people with rural backgrounds. The smell of earth varies with conditions and soil types and helps soil scientists classify the types. For this activity the young scientists will be using their sense of smell to determine differences in soil and will be introduced to the changes that occur when water is added to soil. The terms adults use to describe odors have taken years of experience to assimilate. Exposing children to the experiences of differentiating between soil types or conditions can increase their awareness of their sense of smell.

Before the Activity

Ask the children to prepare the activity sites by spreading out newsprint. Tell them to use the trays to contain the mess. Set out the containers of the soils. Divide the class into small groups.

What to Do

1. Have each group put a spoonful of each kind of soil into individual cups, two cups for each soil type. Have them mark each pair of cups containing the same soil type with the same color.

2. Ask the children to smell the soil samples. Ask: Do they all smell the same? If not, how are they different?

C▪O▪N▪N▪E▪C▪T▪I▪O▪N▪S

To Language

Expressive Language - Children will use words and comparisons to describe the differences in the soils they are smelling.

To Math

Counting and Measuring - Children might count drops to measure the water added to the sample or the volume of the soil sample.

Science Concept

Rocks have unique physical properties, and these properties can be used for classification.

Science Process Skill

To focus observations by using the senses.

Science Vocabulary

clay
dry
earth
musty
sand
soil
sour
sweet
wet

3. Tell the children to add water to one of each type of soil sample, drop by drop, and to smell carefully for any changes. You might have the children count drops as they add the water.

4. Next ask them to compare the smell of the wet samples to the dry samples. Garden soil may have a noticeable difference in smell, while sand may have little difference.

5. Encourage the children to talk about how the smells are different, which smells they like better, and why. Encourage children to describe how the soils smell. They may have to make comparisons to other odors that they are already familiar with: "This wet soil smells like my grandma's garden."

6. Have the children pour all the samples into a single container. As a group, select an appropriate location on the school grounds to place the soil. Discuss the important issues of soil loss and erosion and the need for caring for the environment.

Assessing the Activity

Do the children notice differences between the wet and dry samples? Do they exhibit a growing understanding of and ability to use descriptive words? Do they clearly indicate similarities and differences?

ACTIVITY 6

Up Goes One, Down Goes the Other

Materials

1 container each of clay, sand, potting soil, and playground soil

newsprint

spoons

double-pan balance (per group)

small cups (4 per group)

This activity incorporates the use of the balance. The task is to compare the mass of each different type of soil sample in a formalized way and it teaches the accurate use of the balance. The children also will learn to control sample size.

What to Do

1. Show the children how to fill the cups and place them on the balance pans for comparison. Impress upon the children the importance of always filling the cups level full. This will introduce them to the idea of making consistent comparisons. They will not fully understand the concept, but it is important to model good scientific procedures. Once you have demonstrated the process, children will be able to do the activity in small groups.

2. Have the children work in groups to prepare four cups, each filled with a different soil type.

3. Have the children compare the samples by using the balance. Then have them place the cups in order from the heaviest to the lightest.

C ▪ O ▪ N ▪ N ▪ E ▪ C ▪ T ▪ I ▪ O ▪ N ▪ S

To Language

Expressive Language - Children will use the terms *greater than* and *less than* when using the balance. (Now is an excellent time for you to reinforce for the correct use of these qualitative terms.)

To Math

Measuring and Comparing - Children will determine which soil samples have the greater mass and which have the lesser mass. Children will learn to measure equal volumes of solid materials.

Science Concept

Soils have unique physical properties, and soil is an important component of the natural world.

Science Process Skill

To focus observations by using the senses.

Science Vocabulary

balance
greater than
heavy
less than
light

Assessing the Activity

Have the children observe as you place samples on the balance pans. The children should be able to correctly state which side of the balance holds the sample that is heavier or lighter than the other sample.

ACTIVITY 7

It's All Wet

Materials

1 container each of clay, sand, potting soil, and playground soil

newsprint

spoons

small cups

toothpicks

droppers

water

It is important for young scientists to be able to observe the characteristics of change. This activity focuses on the change that occurs when water is mixed with soil. Children are actively involved in changing materials and in observing how the change is brought about. They will begin to transfer their understanding of this process to other experiences.

Before the Activity

You have the choice of bringing soil samples into the classroom or taking the class on a field trip to collect them. The amount of clay or humus in a sample will affect its ability to absorb water and to be formed into and hold the shape of a ball. A variety of samples will allow children to see the differences in soils. Be prepared: This is a messy activity.

What to Do

1. Select one of the soil samples. Have each child spoon a small amount into a cup. Invite the children to look at, smell, and feel the soil, and to describe their observations. Careful observation establishes a base of information.

C ▪ O ▪ N ▪ N ▪ E ▪ C ▪ T ▪ I ▪ O ▪ N ▪ S

To Language

Expressive Language - Children will use the science vocabulary to describe what happens to soil sample as water is added.

To Math

Counting and Measuring - Children might use these skills when adding drops of water to soil samples.

Science Concept

Soils have unique physical properties, and soil is an important component of the natural world.

Science Process Skill

To focus observations by using the senses.

Science Vocabulary

absorb
clay
dry
humus
moist
soil
stir
wet

2. Direct them to add a small amount of water drop by drop to their soil sample and to repeat their previous observations. You might have the children count as they add the drops. Adding water and stirring cause a physical change to occur. Talk with the children about how the dry and wet soils are different.

3. Have the children add water until the sample is saturated and stir the soil with a toothpick until the water is in all parts of the soil. Ask for their observations.

4. Divide the class into small groups of four and repeat the process with each of the soil types. (You may want to label and save these wet soil samples for the next activity.)

5. Send home Rocks and Soil Family Connection Activity 3 (page 287).

Assessing the Activity

Children's discussion will indicate to what extent they are observing differences and similarities due to the addition of water to the soil samples.

ACTIVITY 8

Drying out Dirt

Materials

waxed paper or plastic foam deli trays

newsprint

wet soil samples (from the previous activity) or fresh samples

various tools to shape and form wet soil, such as spoons and sticks

Making mud pies just seems to go with childhood. In the previous activity, the children made the mud. Now they will make the pies. They will experience the effects of water on various soil types and the changes that occur as soils dry.

Before the Activity

Wet soil samples from the previous activity will work perfectly here (rewet them if necessary). If these are not available, make fresh tubs of various wet soils. Sand will not hold together well but should be included to enable the children to observe differences.

C▪O▪N▪N▪E▪C▪T▪I▪O▪N▪S

To Language

Expressive Language - Children will talk about what they made from wet soil samples, whether it was easy or difficult to sculpt with the wet soil, how they completed their creation, and how it is similar to or different from the soils they used in the previous activity.

Science Concept

Soils have unique physical properties, and soil is an important component of the natural world.

Science Process Skill

To focus observations by using the senses.

Science Vocabulary

compact
dry
evaporate
loose
moist
soil names
wet

What to Do

1. Tell the children to empty a small container of wet soil onto a sheet of waxed paper or a plastic foam tray.

2. Have them sculpture their soils into any shape they want.

3. Allow the samples to dry. Depending on the humidity, this may take overnight or several days.

4. Let the children observe each dried sample. Ask: Does it resemble the mud or soil you began working with?

5. Ask: Can you do something to make it look like the original soil? Let them try their ideas. Do they work?

Assessing the Activity

Each child should be able to recognize the wet and dry soil samples as being samples of the original soil type, such as wet clay and dry clay and an original clay sample.

ACTIVITY 9

Making Soil

Materials

nonstandard units such as cubes or washers

large, labeled containers of sand, clay, and humus

spoons

double-pan balance

several small containers, such as cups or paper bags (per group)

plastic trays

paper and tape for labels

pieces of sandstone and shale (optional)

Soil is a mixture of sand, clay, and humus. Sand and clay come from the breakup of parent rocks, and humus from decaying animal and plant remains. This activity provides children with the firsthand experience of how soil is produced.

Before the Activity

Prepare labeled containers of sand, clay, and humus, and place them in a central location.

What to Do

1. Discuss with children that soil is a mixture of sand, clay, and humus. Optional: Demonstrate how sandstone and shale can be rubbed together to produce loose sand and clay. These products may be added to small amounts of humus to create some homemade soil.

C▪O▪N▪N▪E▪C▪T▪I▪O▪N▪S

To Language

Expressive Language - Children will apply the soil science vocabulary they have acquired when they discuss their soil.

Written Language - Children will make labels for their soil containers by copying labels, at their level of development, from the larger, labeled containers.

To Math

Measuring - Children will use the balance with nonstandard units to compare the sand, clay, and humus mixture they create or use small cups to measure and compare their components by volume.

Science Concept

Soils have unique physical properties, and soil is an important component of the natural world.

Science Process Skill

To focus observations by using the senses.

Science Vocabulary

clay
equal
humus
sand
soil

2. Demonstrate to the children how to use the balance to measure equal masses (weights) of sand, clay, and humus.

3. Allow children to work in groups of two or four to mix their own soil samples. Tell them to start with equal amounts (weights) of sand, clay, and humus, but let them try some of their own ratios.

4. Have children label their soil samples with their names. (Save these samples for the next activity.)

Assessing the Activity

Observe children as they measure to create their mixtures. Ask them to describe the mixture of rocks, clay, and humus they used to make their soil.

ACTIVITY 10

Using Soil

Materials (per group)

planting containers

homemade soil (from the previous activity)

assortment of seeds that grow quickly, such as peas, beans, corn, radish, and marigolds

paper, crayons, and tape for labels

This activity enables children to make practical use of the soil samples created in the previous activity and can provide the classroom with a variety of plants for use in the Plants unit. Soil is a mixture in which seeds may be sown and plants grown. It is a powerful experience for children to make the connection between soil and plants.

What to Do

1. Have the children work in their groups from the previous activity.

2. Direct each child to choose one of their containers of soil from the previous activity and a variety of seeds. Suggest that within the group they use a variety of seeds so a diverse group of plants will grow.

3. Demonstrate proper planting and watering techniques.

4. Help children add labels with names, pictures, or actual seeds they have planted to the soil label already on their containers. Emphasize the importance of careful labeling to ensure later identification.

C ■ O ■ N ■ N ■ E ■ C ■ T ■ I ■ O ■ N ■ S

To Language

Expressive Language - This activity requires children to link events. Their discussion should include the combining of two concepts: We made soil from . . . , and we grew plants in our soil mixture.

Discovery Journals - Children will return to previous Discovery Journal entries and add drawings of the growing plants.

Written Language - Children will label containers.

Science Concept

Soils have unique physical properties, and soil is an important component of the natural world.

Science Process Skill

To focus observations by using the senses.

Science Vocabulary

grow
leaves
plants
roots
seeds
soil
sprout
stems

5. Have children return to previous Discovery Journal entries and add drawings of the growing plants in their soil samples.

Assessing the Activity

Over the next several days, discuss with children what is taking place. Can they draw a picture of what happens when seeds are planted in the soil and water is added? The Plants unit will build on these initial discoveries.

CHECKPOINT

Soil for My Garden

Materials

small paper bags (1 per child)

large spoons

clear plastic tub

large containers of sand, clay, and humus (from Focusing Observations Activity 9, Making Soil, page 100)

This activity will give you the opportunity to assess each child's knowledge of the composition and various types of soil. The practice provided by the repetition will give reinforcement to children who need it. This activity provides a nice connection to the Plants unit.

Before the Activity

Place the containers of soils in a central location.

What to Do

1. Gather the children into a circle. Tell them that you are getting ready to plant a garden but that you need their help in preparing the soil.

2. Hand one child a paper bag and a spoon. Say: I need some clay. Please go to the container of clay and put a spoonful of the clay into this bag.

3. If the child chooses correctly, empty the contents into the plastic tub. If not, describe clay to the child and send her or him back to find some for you.

C ▪ O ▪ N ▪ N ▪ E ▪ C ▪ T ▪ I ▪ O ▪ N ▪ S

To Language

Semantics - Children will demonstrate their new-found understanding of soil types and the importance of those types as they help you prepare soil for a garden.

Expressive Language - Children will use the labels of the different soil types as they tell you what type of soil needs to be added.

Science Concept

Soils have unique physical properties, and soil is an important component of the natural world.

Science Process Skill

To focus observations by using the senses.

Science Vocabulary

clay
humus
sand
soil

4. Go on to the next child, this time asking that she or he bring you some humus or sand. Give each child a turn in helping you prepare the soil.

5. From time to time ask the children to tell you what type of soil you need more of. Check for correct use of terms.

Assessing the Activity

Observe the children's ability to select the appropriate soil-making materials.

ACTIVITY 1

Where Does This Rock Belong?

Materials

rocks (small enough to fit in an egg carton compartment)

egg carton or ice cube tray (1 per child or group)

Discovery Journals

Once children are able to recognize similarities and differences among objects, they should be encouraged to take the next step in mastery of grouping skills: to recognize an individual object as being part of an established set. This activity challenges children to identify members of sets of rocks.

Before the Activity

Gather two large sets of rocks with obvious contrast in color (light/dark), and divide them among the egg cartons so that each child will have a variety of light and dark rocks.

What to Do

1. Provide the children with their 12-rock carrier. Ask them to separate their rocks into light and dark groups by putting all of the light rocks on one side of the carrier and all the dark rocks on the other side.

C·O·N·N·E·C·T·I·O·N·S

To Language

Expressive Language - Children will recognize that not all rocks are the same and use the science vocabulary in talking about the difference in their properties.

Discovery Journals - Children will record how they divided their rocks by light and dark colors. Some may label the new rocks with the words *light* or *dark*. Other children may use colored marks to indicate the groupings.

To Math

Grouping - Children will divide one large group into two smaller groups by the property of color.

Science Concept

Rocks have unique physical properties, and these properties can be used for classification.

Science Process Skill

To use observations to classify.

Science Vocabulary

dark
group
light
rock names

2. Provide additional rocks and ask children to place them into the correct group.

3. Ask the children to explain why they placed the new rocks where they did.

4. Help the children write words or symbols in their Discovery Journals for the characteristics of the rocks in the two groups; in this example, dark and light. Have them record the number of rocks in each group. Then have them place new rocks in the correct group according to this classification scheme.

Assessing the Activity

Are the children able to separate their rocks into distinct groups?

ACTIVITY 2

Some Rocks Are Alike

Materials

rocks (small enough to fit in an egg carton compartment)

egg carton or ice cube tray (1 per child or group)

Like animals and plants, rocks have characteristics that allow us to classify them into groups. Although it is easy to focus on a single attribute that makes one rock different from another, children may not as easily see that rocks have many attributes that are the same. This activity asks the children to observe a set of rocks and to sort them into sets by similar characteristics. This is a more complex task than the simple sorting into two groups because the children are sorting the same set in several different ways.

Before the Activity

The collection of rocks must have enough distinct characteristics so that the first groupings can be made easily. The rocks should be similar enough that only two choices can be made in each grouping, not three or four.

What to Do

1. Provide the children with egg carton carriers containing a variety of rocks.

C·O·N·N·E·C·T·I·O·N·S

To Language

Expressive Language - Children will begin using the science vocabulary as they select an attribute and group their rocks accordingly. (As an awareness of the variety of rock characteristics begins to develop, so will the children's expressive language skills.)

To Math

Grouping - Children will begin experimenting with grouping rocks according to different characteristics.

Science Concept

Rocks have unique physical properties, and these properties can be used for classification.

Science Process Skill

To use observations to classify.

Science Vocabulary

descriptive words of rock characteristics (such as size, shape, weight, texture, and color)
rock names

2. Ask them to look at the rocks carefully. Ask: What colors are your rocks? What do your rocks feel like? What shapes are your rocks?

3. Focus the children on a single property, such as rough versus smooth. Ask them to put all of the rough rocks on one side of the egg carton and all the smooth rocks on the other side.

4. Follow the same procedure for another property, such as shape, size, or color.

5. Encourage the children to identify as many different rock properties as they can, then to create groups accordingly.

Assessing the Activity

It will be interesting for you to note the developmental levels of the children, as some will only be able to determine one characteristic, and others will be able to make many different groups from the same rocks. Have the children describe their selected properties and the resulting groups.

ACTIVITY 3

Which Rock Is the Longest?

Materials (per child or group)

6 rocks of different lengths (flat rocks work best)

nonstandard unit of length, such as interlocking cubes or paper clips

Discovery Journals

Length is a basic quantitative unit. This activity asks children to use a nonstandard unit to determine the lengths of the rocks in a collection and then to rank order the rocks from the longest to the shortest. The smaller the measuring unit selected, the more accurate the children can be.

Before the Activity

Prepare a rock collection by selecting rocks of obviously different sizes, yet with some very close in size. Try to choose rocks as close to a whole interlocking-cube increment (or other unit of length) as possible.

What to Do

1. Ask the children to look carefully at their rocks and to talk about what is alike and what is different. They likely will notice the difference in length. If not, call their attention to this property.

C ▪ O ▪ N ▪ N ▪ E ▪ C ▪ T ▪ I ▪ O ▪ N ▪ S

To Language

Expressive Language - Children will practice their science vocabulary. (Encourage children to use their words as they explain why they ordered their rocks as they did.)

Discovery Journals - Children will record the order of their numbered rocks.

To Math

Ordering - Children will order rocks by length.

Measuring - Children will learn how to measure the length of an object by using a nonstandard unit of length.

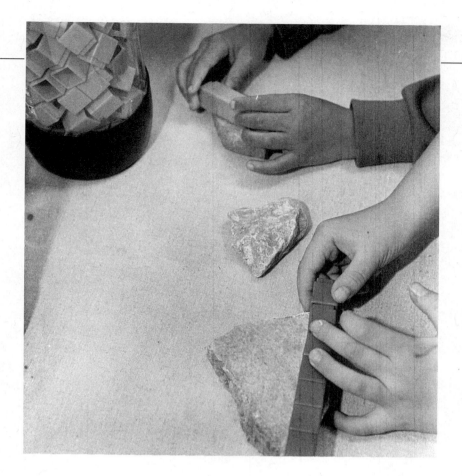

Science Concept

Rocks have unique physical properties, and these properties can be used for classification.

Science Process Skill

To use observations to classify.

Science Vocabulary

long
longer
longest
measure
order
short
shorter
shortest

2. Invite the children to measure the length of the different rocks and to line them up in order of length.

3. Have the children trace around the rocks in their sets and record the measurements in their Discovery Journals. They can draw pictures of blocks to represent each measurement, write the numerals, or both.

4. Send home Rocks and Soil Family Connection Activity 4 (page 287).

Assessing the Activity

Observe the accuracy of children's rank ordering of the rocks according to length. Rocks that are very similar in size may be used to evaluate the children. Their reasons for placing the rocks in the correct order by length will tell you whether they are using the concept correctly.

ACTIVITY 4

How Massive Is a Rock?

Materials

rocks

egg carton or ice cube tray (per group)

standard mass (see Before the Activity)

double-pan balance

One of the quantitative characteristics of an object is its mass. Mass is the quantity of matter and usually is measured in grams or kilograms. Your children can learn to recognize when to use the word *mass*. For them it is any time they use a balance. This activity uses a simple binary classification of *greater than* or *less than* to group rocks.

Before the Activity

Order the rocks you've selected by mass. Then find an object, such as block or a small jar of washers, that has a mass between the two middle rocks. Use this object as the standard mass for this activity. The masses of the rocks will be either greater than or less than this object. Place several different rocks into each rock carrier.

C·O·N·N·E·C·T·I·O·N·S

To Language

Expressive Language - This activity will introduce the children to words other than *heavier* and *lighter*: *greater than* and *less than*. They will find this exciting, as the vocabulary sounds quite "grown up." You might even tell them that scientists use these words.

To Math

Weighing and Comparing - Children will use a balance to determine whether rocks are of greater or lesser mass than a standard.

Science Concept

Rocks have unique physical properties, and these properties can be used for classification.

Science Process Skill

To use observations to classify.

Science Vocabulary

balance
equal
greater than
less than
mass
rock names

What to Do

1. Review with the children how to use the balance to compare mass.

2. Give the children the standard mass and the egg cartons.

3. Have the children classify their rocks according to whether a rock's mass is greater or less than the standard mass. Use the terms *greater than* and *less than* as you talk with the children. Have them put the "greater-than" rocks on one side of the carton and the "less-than" rocks on the other side.

Assessing the Activity

Compare your results with the children's results. Are they showing increased mastery in their work at comparing masses?

ACTIVITY 5

Order of Mass

Materials (per group)

double-pan balance
3 numbered rocks
additional rocks
Discovery Journals

Ordering a set of rocks by using a balance requires more skill than simply dividing them into two groups. Each measurement asks the children to make comparisons between two rocks. Asking the children to order a dozen rocks by mass requires many uses of the balance. As the balance becomes a familiar tool, the idea of mass as an attribute of objects is instilled.

Before the Activity

Choose the rocks depending on the sophistication of the children; the closer the rocks are in mass, the more accurate the children must be in their use of the balance. Number the set of the rocks from 1 to 3, and determine and record the mass of each rock in the set. Select additional rocks of a variety of masses and place them into the egg cartons.

C▪O▪N▪N▪E▪C▪T▪I▪O▪N▪S

To Language

Expressive Language - Children will continue practicing their use of the science vocabulary.

Discovery Journals - Children will record the numbers of their rocks in rank order.

Semantics - When children are successful in determining the mass of and ordering their rocks, they have reached a level of true understanding of the concept and the language of order.

To Math

Weighing - Children will refine their skills with the balance.

Ordering - Children will practice rank ordering objects according to how the objects compare to each other.

Science Concept

Rocks have unique physical properties, and these properties can be used for classification.

Science Process Skill

To use observations to classify.

Science Vocabulary

balance
greater than
less than
mass
order
rock names

What to Do

1. Hand out the sets of rocks and the balances.

2. Have the children use the balance to find the most massive rock.

3. Continue this process until the children have rank ordered all three rocks according to mass.

4. Have them trace the rocks in order of mass into their Discovery Journals.

Assessing the Activity

Do your observations of the children at work indicate that they understand the process of rank ordering? Do the Discovery Journal entries indicate an accurate understanding of classifying by mass? Give each group a new rock. Can they place it in the correct order with the other three rocks?

ACTIVITY 6

Cover Me Up

Materials (per group)

sheets of paper
rocks of various sizes

The two-dimensional space that an object takes up is called *area*. An object's area can be described in standard units, such as square meters, or in nonstandard units. In this activity children are asked to compare the area of rocks to the areas of a small and a large circle.

Before the Activity

Select a variety of different-sized rocks for this activity. Flat rocks will be the easiest for children to use and observe.

What to Do

1. Introduce the concept of *area* by demonstrating to the children that every rock covers a certain amount of space. First, draw a small and large circle, side by side, on a sheet of paper. Then select a small and a large rock and use them to show the children that the large rock can cover the areas of both circles but the smaller rock can only cover the area of the small circle.

C▪O▪N▪N▪E▪C▪T▪I▪O▪N▪S

To Language

Expressive Language - Children will compare the area of rocks and use the science vocabulary with their partners and with you as they explain their groupings and the surface area the rocks cover.

To Math

Sorting, Classifying, and Comparing - Children will use these skills as they sort rocks according to size, classify them into large or small groups, and compare surface area covered by the rocks.

Science Concept

Rocks have unique physical properties, and these properties can be used for classification.

Science Process Skill

To use observations to classify.

Science Vocabulary

area
large
small
surface

2. Have the children draw a large and small circle side by side.

3. Distribute a variety of rocks to each group.

4. Tell the children to find rocks that will cover both circles. Then tell them to find rocks that fit inside the big circle. Ask: Can you find rocks that fit inside the small circle? What about rocks that fit inside the large circle but still cover the small circle?

5. Continue to explore different combinations of rock sizes. Challenge the children to start grouping their rocks according to the surface area they cover and their relationship to the two circles.

6. Challenge the children to discover a way that the large circle can be covered with only small rocks.

Assessing the Activity

Observe the accuracy with which children select appropriately sized rocks. Have them demonstrate that the rocks they have selected have the approximate surface area of the circle they selected.

ACTIVITY 7

Let's Find the Biggest and Smallest Rocks

Materials (per group)

several (more than 5) rocks in a variety of sizes

Another important attribute of any rock is the space it takes up—its volume. Scientists measure volume in several units, such as in liters or cubic centimeters. Although this activity does not ask children to quantify to that degree, it is important that they begin to recognize volume as a measurement. Children often mix up the concepts of length, area, and volume. They frequently look at only one dimension, such as length, to determine size.

What to Do

1. Provide each group of three or four children with several rocks.

2. Ask the children to explore the rocks. Have them observe how long, high, and wide the rocks are. Demonstrate by holding different rocks side by side so children can make comparisons. Encourage them to find big, small, and medium-size rocks and group them into three piles.

3. Ask the children to take a rock from each group and rank order them: small, medium, and large.

C ▪ O ▪ N ▪ N ▪ E ▪ C ▪ T ▪ I ▪ O ▪ N ▪ S

To Language

Expressive Language - Children will use the science vocabulary as they question each other about the order in which they place their rocks.

To Math

Ordering - Children will order rocks according to size.

Science Concept

Rocks have unique physical properties, and these properties can be used for classification.

Science Process Skill

To use observations to classify.

Science Vocabulary

biggest
medium
order
rock names
size
smallest

4. Once the children have mastered rank ordering three rocks, have them mix up the rocks and choose five rocks of varying size. Challenge the children to place the rocks in rank order.

5. Ask the children to check each other's orders and to explain their own.

Assessing the Activity

Are the children successful in rank ordering a variety of rocks? Observe the children as they organize their rocks according to the rocks' varying volumes. Discuss with them why they placed their rocks in a particular order.

CHECKPOINT

My Rock Is . . .

Materials

rocks
Discovery Journals

This activity encourages children to combine their observing and classifying skills to describe a special rock they choose themselves. Encourage them to be detailed and specific so that they really tell all they can about their rock.

What to Do

1. Ask the children to describe ways the rocks are alike and different. Review all of the ways they have classified rocks, such as size, length, area, color, texture, and mass. Encourage the children to use the vocabulary words as they describe their rocks.

2. Have each child select a special rock to feature in his or her Discovery Journal. Say: Think of as many ways can to describe your rock. Encourage the children to use the skills that they have learned in the last several activities. You may need to offer suggestions for some children.

C▪O▪N▪N▪E▪C▪T▪I▪O▪N▪S

To Language

Expressive Language - Children will practice the science vocabulary of all the rock activities that investigated size, length, area, color, texture, and mass.

Discovery Journals - Children will record information about their selected rock at their own writing level. Children should be encouraged to refer to other Discovery Journal entries for ideas.

To Math

Comparing - Children will use comparative language as they describe their selected rock. (This gives you the opportunity to assess their understanding of this language.)

Science Concept

Rocks have unique physical properties, and these properties can be used for classification.

Science Process Skill

To use observations to classify.

Science Vocabulary

biggest
longest
rock attributes, such as shiny/dull, rough/smooth, big/small, long/round
rock names
shortest

3. Encourage the children to be creative. They may want to draw, make rubbings, write with their own invented spelling, or draw a picture of the rock on the balance. You may be surprised at the ways they decide to organize and use the classification skills they have learned.

4. You may want to have the children make a special *My Rock Is . . .* book.

Assessing the Activity

Discuss with each child what makes his or her rock special. Can they discuss their rock's unique properties? Ask the child to locate a rock from the classroom collection that has similar characteristics to those of the child's special rock.

Shake, Rattle, and Roll

ADDITIONAL STIMULATION

Materials

several rocks
opaque container with lid

This activity allows you to work with children who are having trouble identifying some of the attributes of rocks. As it is a game, it is a fun way to extend and enhance the classification ideas being taught. Once the game has been introduced, the children will be able to play it on their own.

Before the Activity

In this activity you will be "rolling" rocks from the container onto a table. Choose a group of four to six rocks (two or three rock attribute pairs) for each roll. Examples of attribute pairs: big-small, long-short, color-color, shiny-dull, smooth-sharp, rough-smooth, light-heavy, round-oblong.

What to Do

1. Select a child to be the rock hound. Put a group of rocks into the container, and cover the container. (Select the rocks to classify according to each child's ability. For example, one child might be given a group of pink rocks and black rocks to classify by color. A more skilled child may be given a more complex task.)

C · O · N · N · E · C · T · I · O · N · S

To Language

Semantics - The child who is the "rock hound" will demonstrate his or her level of understanding by how well he or she masters the activity. Not all children will have the same level of understanding, and that is perfectly acceptable.

Science Concept

Rocks have unique physical properties, and these properties can be used for classification.

Science Process Skill

To use observations to classify.

Science Vocabulary

rock attribute words (see Before the Activity)

rock names

2. As the children chant "Shake, rattle, and roll," you shake the container, rattle it, remove the lid, and roll out the rocks in front of the selected child.

3. Tell the "rock hound" to classify the rocks into groups as quickly as possible. (Do not give away the attribute by which you selected the rocks.) Speed and excitement add to the fun of the game.

4. Ask the rock hound to explain how the rocks are alike and how they are different.

Assessing the Activity

Observe each child's performance in the game. Can the child correctly classify the rocks according to an appropriate attribute?

ACTIVITY 1

What Works Best?

Materials

rock (1 per child)
large sheets of newsprint
crayons

There are many ways to communicate information about the same set of objects. People choose different methods for different reasons. Some are more effective and more easily understood than others. This activity makes that fact obvious.

Before the Activity

Tape sheets of newsprint to a wall.

What to Do

1. Place the rocks in a bucket or other container. Pass it around and have each child choose a rock.

2. Ask one child to choose a word that describes his or her rock, such as rough. Ask the other children: If your rock is not rough, what is it? (smooth)

C▪O▪N▪N▪E▪C▪T▪I▪O▪N▪S

To Language

Expressive Language - Children will use their expressive skills and the science vocabulary as they talk about the different ways rocks can be described. This is a good time to encourage children's use of opposites.

To Math

Charting and Graphing - Children will compare the usefulness of different methods of recording information.

3. On one of the sheets of newsprint, write *rough* at the top left and *smooth* at the top right. Draw a line down the center.

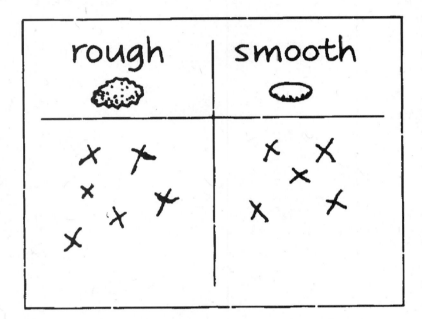

Science Concept

Rocks have unique physical properties, and these properties can be used for classification.

Science Process Skill

To organize and communicate observations.

Science Vocabulary

descriptive words of the various physical attributes of the rocks, such as rough, round, and black

4. Ask each child to make a mark somewhere on the correct side of the paper for his or her rock.

5. Ask: Which do we have more of, rough rocks or smooth rocks? It will be obvious to the children that they will have to count or do something else besides just look at the chart. What do they suggest? Can they come up with a way, such as a bar graph, that communicates clearly which group has more?

6. Have another child give another characteristic, and have the class try the new method for organizing the class's data. Discuss the results with the children. Which method made it easiest for them to tell which group had more?

Assessing the Activity

Can the children readily tell which group has more rocks of a certain characteristic by observing the displays of data?

ACTIVITY 2

Paper Graphs, People Graphs

In this activity the children participate in the construction of two bar graphs. First they sort themselves into two columns according to a property of their rocks. They then learn to record this information on paper by coloring squares in columns.

Materials

rocks (1 per child)
large sheets of newsprint or large sheets of graph paper
Discovery Journals

Before the Activity

Select rocks that are obviously light and dark and rough and smooth. You may want to prepare blank bar graphs, rather than doing it as part of the activity.

What to Do

1. Pass out one rock to each child. Ask children to decide whether their rocks are light or dark.

2. Have the children with light rocks form a line on one side of you and the children with dark rocks form a line on your other side. In unison with the children, count the members of each line.

3. Ask: How could we show someone who is not in the room how many light rocks we have and how many dark rocks we have?

C·O·N·N·E·C·T·I·O·N·S

To Language

Expressive Language - Children will use their expressive skills and the science vocabulary as they talk about the rock attributes and tell how they know which group has more members.

Discovery Journals - Children's drawings will communicate something about their experience.

To Math

Graphing - Children will explore one method of recording information, the bar graph.

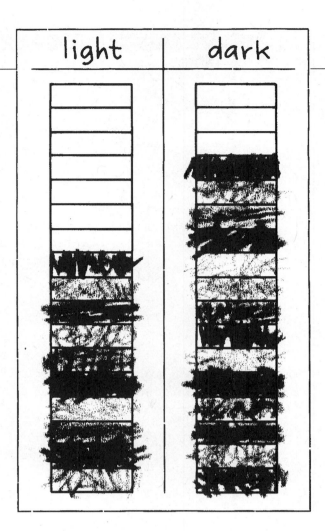

light	dark

Science Concept

Rocks have unique physical properties, and these properties can be used for classification.

Science Process Skill

To organize and communicate observations.

Science Vocabulary

bar graph

counting words such as less, longest, more, shortest

descriptive words of physical attributes of rocks, such as light, dark, smooth, rough

4. Suggest that they work with you to make a bar graph. Make two columns on graph paper or use the blank bar graph you prepared earlier. Label one column Light and the other column Dark. Have each child color in a square in the correct column, using appropriate colors.

5. Ask the children to look at the bar graph and tell you whether there are more light or more dark rocks. Ask: How do you know? Some may count, and others may just state which bar is the longest.

6. Repeat the process using the attributes rough and smooth.

7. Ask the children to draw something in their Discovery Journals to tell about the dark and light rocks or the rough and smooth rocks. Some children will want to add numerals or labels to their drawings.

Assessing the Activity

Can the children look at the bar graphs and tell which group has more?

CHECKPOINT

Shiny or Dull?

Materials

5 or 6 numbered rocks, some shiny and some dull (per group)
Discovery Journals

Luster, or shininess, is not a difficult attribute to classify, but it is an important rock science concept. Galena (lead ore) has a shiny, metallic luster. Mica has a pearly luster. Quartz, agate, obsidian, and coal display luster, while sandstone and limestone are usually not shiny. Glassy, waxy, brilliant, silky, greasy, and dull are other ways to describe luster.

Before the Activity

Decide whether this activity will be done individually or in groups of four. Prepare the correct number of rock sets, each containing five or six rocks. Select rocks on the basis of luster and number each one.

C•O•N•N•E•C•T•I•O•N•S

To Language

Expressive Language - Children will recognize a new characteristic of rocks and to practice labeling rocks as either shiny or dull. (Eventually children will be able to tell degrees of shininess or dullness. Practice makes perfect.)

Discovery Journals - Children will record their findings.

To Math

Grouping - Children will separate rock specimens into two groups according to luster.

Charting - Children will record results on a chart.

Ordering - Children will rank order rocks by luster.

What to Do

1. Distribute the rocks to the groups or place them in the Discovery Center.

2. Ask the children to separate the rocks into groups of shiny and dull and then to record the number of the rocks on a chart they have created in their Discovery Journals.

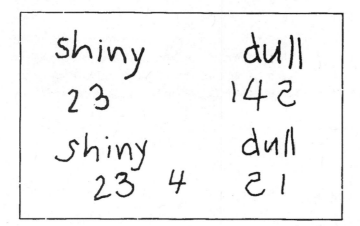

3. Request that the children rank order their rocks from dullest to shiniest and record this information on another chart in their Discovery Journals.

Assessing the Activity

Check the children's results in their Discovery Journals. Have they clearly and accurately communicated which rocks are shiny and which are dull?

Science Concept

Rocks have unique physical properties, and these properties can be used for classification.

Science Process Skill

To organize and communicate observations.

Science Vocabulary

chart
dull
luster
order
shiny

ADDITIONAL STIMULATION

Kerplunk!

Materials

large paper or plastic measuring chart
newsprint
rocks of differing sizes (1 per child)
shallow plastic tub of water
measuring chart for recording the results (1 per child)
large sheet of paper to graph the results
sponge
access to water (for refilling the tub)
Discovery Journals

If you were standing next to a mountain lake and a rock came falling down the mountainside, headed for the lake, could you tell whether the water was going to splash you? That question will be explored this activity. You see, the bigger the rock, the bigger the splash. Kerplunk! can be done as a small- or large-group activity. The children will be absolutely delighted either way.

Before the Activity

Make a measuring chart, large enough to accommodate the tub. With a permanent marker, draw concentric circles on the chart. Prepare a small replica of the chart, and photocopy it for each child. Prepare the area by spreading out newsprint (or do this activity outdoors).

C▪O▪N▪N▪E▪C▪T▪I▪O▪N▪S

To Language

Expressive Language - Children will predict how far the water will splash, whose rock will splash the farthest, and whose rock will splash the closest to the tub. Lots of language will be exchanged. You will have to listen carefully, because giggling will be going on!

Discovery Journals - Children will use their Discovery Journals to document the splash of their own rocks.

To Math

Charting and Graphing - Children will count the number of circles of the farthest splash their rocks made, record on a class chart, and make a graph showing which rocks splashed the farthest.

Science Concept

Rocks have unique physical properties, and these properties can be used for classification.

Science Process Skill

To organize and communicate observations.

Science Vocabulary

heavy
light
rock names
splash

What to Do

1. Place the tub of water in the center of the measuring chart. Pass out one rock to each child. Instruct the children to drop their rocks into the water one at a time. (Start with the small rocks or the chart will get too wet).

2. Have the children observe the farthest splashes for each rock and record this information on the group measuring chart. Wipe up splashes with a sponge.

3. Have the children trace their rocks in their Discovery Journals and write the number of the farthest circle it splashed. They can do this with one or more rocks.

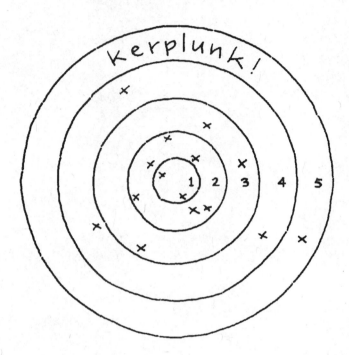

4. As a class, create a large bar graph of the results of all the Kerplunks.

5. Have the children create a bar graph in their own journal for their own rocks.

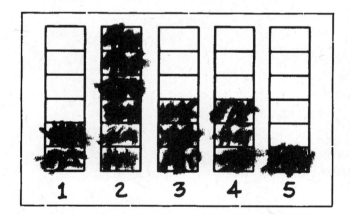

Assessing the Activity

The children should be able to record their own results in their Discovery Journals in both chart and graph form.

UNIT 3

Animals

Essential Information

Most children have a natural attraction to any living thing, particularly to animals. This inherent curiosity is the motivation that generates interest and excitement as the children explore the Discovery Science Animals unit.

It is essential that children realize the importance of animals in the balance of nature. This can best be conveyed by direct experience with a wide variety of animals, since the fragility of many living things cannot be shared with children unless they come into direct contact with them. Although some children are lucky enough to have pets in their homes, many do not. They must rely on school experiences to develop their understanding and attitudes about living things.

Children will display the attitudes about animals they learned from their families. These attitudes may or may not be humane. Children who have fears or dislikes about certain animals will often overcome those attitudes if given the opportunity to do so. Watching other children in a nonthreatening situation will gradually build up a child's courage to work with a disliked animal.

Your role in the classroom is clear. Displaying a caring and humane attitude will have a great impact on the children. No matter how you personally feel about the animals that visit or are necessary for class activities, display only the most positive of attitudes and actions. Choosing not to use a particular animal may be a better choice over exhibiting a negative attitude, which the children will soon discover.

Care of Animals

The Animals unit allows children to add to their knowledge and understanding of animals and to their ability to nurture and care for them. You need to teach the children respect for life and the responsibility that animal adoption entails.

Science Concepts

The following science concepts will be addressed in the Animals unit:

1. Animals display physical and behavioral diversity.
2. Animals are living organisms that breathe, move, grow, and require nourishment.
3. Animals interact with their environment.
4. Animals grow and change throughout their lives.

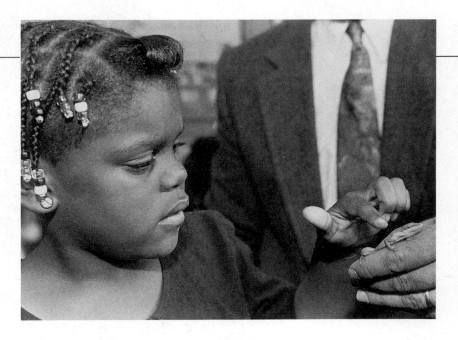

Getting Ready

Add the following materials to the
Discovery Center:

- animals and Animal Discovery
  Collection
- aquariums, cages, jars, and other
  containers for holding animals
  (even a small wading pool for the
  adventurous)
- pictures of animals
- watering bottles
- butterfly kit with growing
  chambers
- yarn
- roll of craft paper or newsprint
- sense cards (see page 137)
- food for animals
- empty boxes (such as shoe boxes)
- dark construction paper
- light source
- magazines with pictures of people
  and animals
- camera and film
- shell collection, including 10 pairs
  of matching shells

Have these materials available for your
use:

- strongly scented liquids such as
  vinegar, vanilla, and peppermint
  essence
- How Heavy Is It? sheet (see page
  138)

Each animal has its own special needs. Numerous books have
been written on the care of the most common pets. You may have
to hunt a bit for information on more exotic animals. Have
people who bring in animals give you clear instructions on how
to care for them. You will need to be able to contact the owner
should questions arise. Ask also that they bring one or more
related books to give you a source of general information on the
animal and its care. Pet shop owners and veterinarians are also
valuable resources.

Wild Animals

Some wild animals are illegal to keep. Most migratory birds fall
into this category, but your state also may make the keeping of
wild mammals illegal. Call your local conservation agency to find
out about your state laws and for the names of local persons who
take care of young or hurt animals. These animal rehabilitation
centers, scattered throughout the country, can serve as excellent
field trip sites. Their job is to heal hurt wild animals, but they
also are interested in educating people on responsibilities toward
wild animals.

Young wild rabbits, squirrels, and mice are all difficult to raise,
so it is best to leave them alone. Some wild creatures, however,
are easy to keep. Spiders and insects are the best examples.
Spiders need live food, mostly insects, to survive. Food for insects
varies from live animals to plant leaves and juices. To keep any
wild creature, you will have to research food and natural habitats.

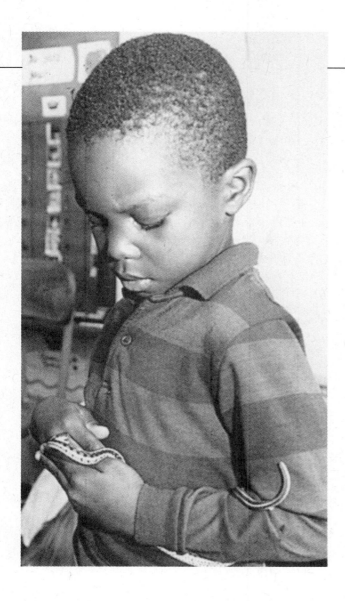

The most environmentally sound method is to bring the specimen in from the wild in the least intrusive manner. Place it into an observation chamber with access to water, allow the children to make their observations, and release it the same day. Have the children participate in returning the wild creatures to freedom, a wonderful and satisfying event.

The Animal Discovery Collection

The Animal Discovery Collection is a group of nonliving animal-related material to be placed in the Discovery Center. The majority of these items should be available to the children for Free Discovery. Place very fragile or small objects, such as delicate coral or tiny fish scales, in a "look, but don't touch" container (such as a stationery box with a clear plastic cover or a plastic box with a magnifier lid).

Following is a list of possible items for the Animal Discovery Collection. Add or delete according to what you have available. Encourage children, family members, and anyone else to add to the collection.

animal hooves (sold as dog chews)

bones

cicada shells

cocoons

coral

dead insects

feathers

fish scales

fossils

fur

galls

hornet or wasp nests

horns

insect eaten bark and leaves

leather

pelts or skins

sand dollars

seashells

skeletons

snail shells

snake skins

sponges

starfish

teeth (from various animals)

turtle shells

You may want to send a letter to families to announce the Animals unit (see the Family Connection, page 288, for an example). Ask them to lend or donate cages, feeders, aquariums, containers, and anything else that might be helpful. Also ask for animals, either as long-term classroom residents or for the One-Week Zoo.

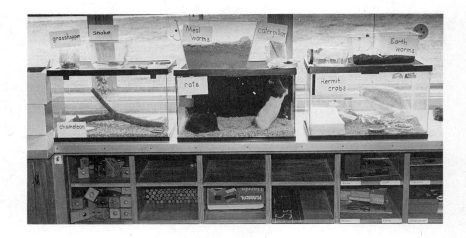

SENSE CARDS

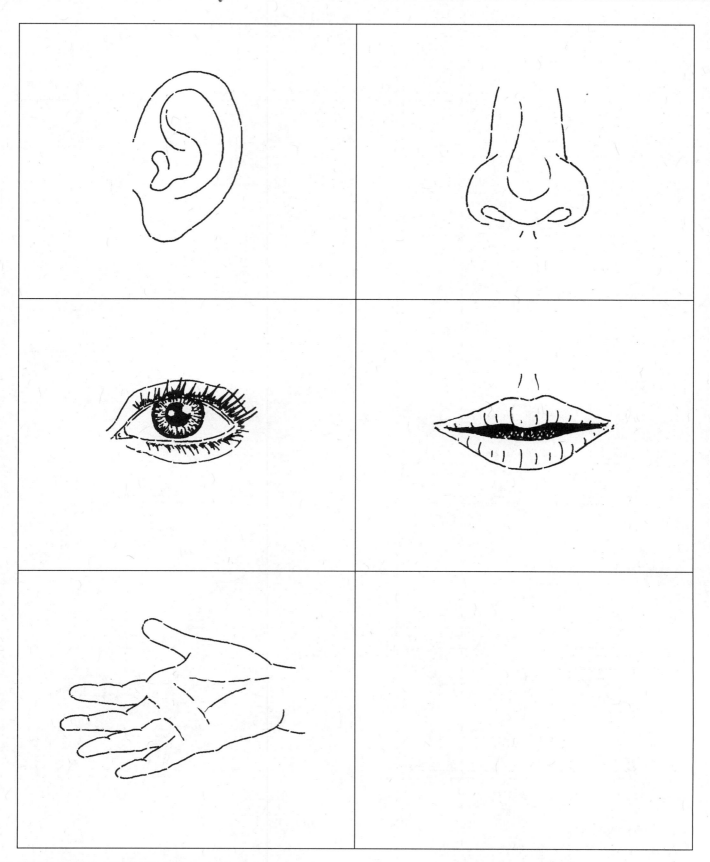

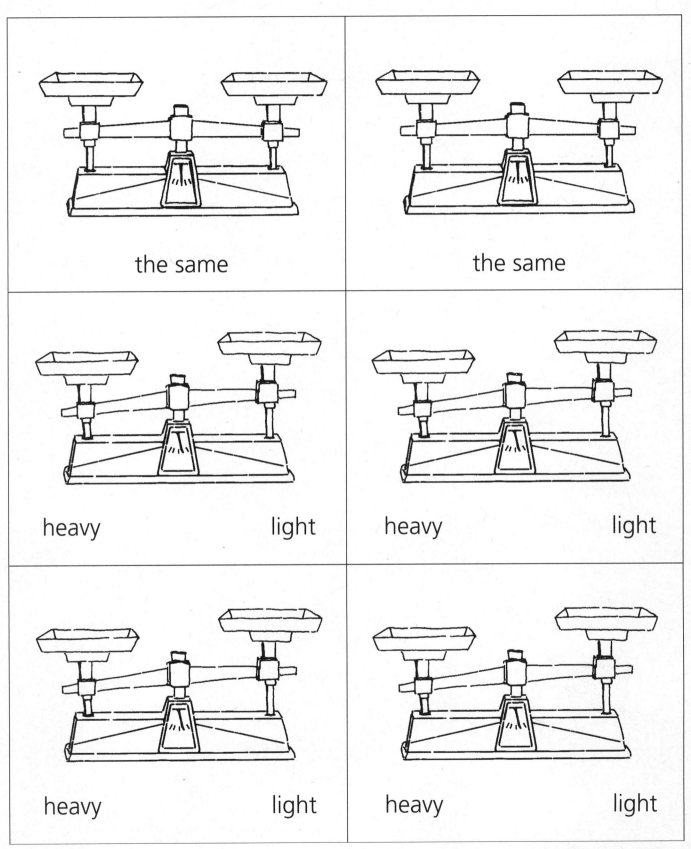

the same   the same

heavy   light   heavy   light

heavy   light   heavy   light

Long-Term Classroom Residents

Long-term classroom residents are animals that will remain in the classroom for the duration of the Animals unit or longer. They should be animals that you are comfortable caring for over a period of time. A variety of animal characteristics should be present. For example, you might have a gerbil, a hermit crab, a goldfish, and some crickets. The following animals are easy to care for as long-term classroom residents. Those that you do not choose as permanent dwellers can be considered for the One-Week Zoo (explained below).

- Small mammals. Hamsters, gerbils, guinea pigs, rabbits
- Insects. Crickets, mealworms, isopods (pill bugs), ants in an ant farm, butterflies (grown from a kit)
- Reptiles. Box turtles, lizards, garden snakes
- Birds. Cockatiels, parakeets, finches
- Others. Fish, snails, tadpoles, spiders, earthworms, hermit crabs

The One-Week Zoo

The One-Week Zoo is a week-long intensive experience with a large variety of animals that gives children the opportunity to interact with all sorts of creatures without committing you to keeping the animals all year. Advance planning with families and others who are willing to share their pets and expertise is very important. This is time well spent, dispersing to many participants the responsibility of providing the experiences with animals that children need. You will not have to provide food and cages, because families and friends will bring everything that is needed with the animal. Care and cleaning will be minimal, because the stay is short. Often the owner will stay with the animal and share information with the children.

Conduct the One-Week Zoo after Free Discovery. You may wish to do the first Activities 1 through 5 and the Checkpoint during the One-Week Zoo.

Following are ideas that may be helpful as you set up the One-Week Zoo:

- Share your plans with other teachers. They may have classroom pets they would be willing to lend.

- Prepare a schedule for visitors. You probably do not want a cat and dog to arrive at the same time. Yet having a German shepherd and a Chihuahua follow each other allows for some interesting comparisons. You will want to accommodate the needs of the pet owners.

- Keep a list of the names, phone numbers, and addresses of your volunteers. You may want to reschedule a visit, ask questions, or write thank-you notes. Family members may be willing to bring a pet the next year, even though their child has moved on.

- Ask an animal shelter volunteer to bring an animal and discuss needs of animals.

- Contact a pet store. You may be able to arrange a field trip to visit or have someone bring animals to the classroom.

Some difficult issues may come up when working with animals. Thinking about these ahead of time will make you better able to handle those situations should they arise.

- Some animals, such as rats and roaches, must be destroyed because they carry disease. This necessity can arise both at home and at school, and should be done as humanely as possible.

- Animals may bite. Children should be taught to avoid startling animals and to handle them gently. Even so, an animal may bite for no apparent reason.

- Some animals are dangerous, though most of us will never come in contact with them, especially in the classroom. These creatures are essential pieces in the complicated jigsaw puzzle of our natural world. The children should have the chance to learn about these animals, with the hope that fear will be replaced with understanding that leads to real tolerance and caring.

- Meat-eating animals must kill for food.

- Living things die. You need to think about your response should this happen in your classroom.

Free Discovery

In the Animals unit, Free Discovery is a wonderful opportunity for both you and the children to explore the diversity of the animal world. Animals can provide a bridge for students to begin to discover the rest of the living world. Placing the animals in the Discovery Center allows the children to become familiar with each animal. Having experience with the Animal Discovery Collection will ready the children for the more complicated observation and classification activities that follow. You may want to use the Success in Science Inventory and Discovery Journal entries to evaluate the children's progress during Free Discovery.

What We Know About Animals

They can be pets.
Some animals run fast.
We need to take care of them.

Some animals are friendly.
Some animals are fat.
Animals are cuddly.
Animals are part of nat

Some animals stay in a cage.
Some animals go to the pound.
You can play with animals.
Some dogs live in a doghouse.

Pets need to eat and to
drink water.
Animals go to a vet.
Some animals can see and
smell better than we can.

Materials

large sheet of newsprint (for a Discovery Chart)

markers

tape

animals

Success in Science Inventory (see page 17)

Discovery Journals

What to Do

1. Bring the children together for discussion and sharing. Prepare a large Discovery Chart entitled What We Know About Animals, and have the children tell you all they know about animals while you record their responses.

2. Begin Free Discovery by introducing the long-term classroom residents and the Animal Discovery Collection.

3. Allow every child the opportunity to spend time in the Discovery Center. Encourage them to write and draw about their discoveries in their Discovery Journals.

4. Record individual performance using the Success in Science Inventory.

5. When the children have had enough time in the Discovery Center, return to the Discovery Chart. Restate the comments recorded on the Discovery Chart, and ask the children to share drawings and writings from their Discovery Journals. Add any new discoveries to the Discovery Chart in a different color. Then ask: What else would you like to learn about animals?

6. At this point, conduct the One-Week Zoo. The One-Week Zoo can be used for the first several activities. (If you have a diverse group of animals, the first several activities may also be done with the long-term classroom residents.)

Story Time

Use this story-telling activity to raise the children's interest in animals.

The Best Pet

Once upon a time there were a brother and a sister, _____ and _____ , who lived with their mother in a very big city. They lived in an apartment with a sign by the elevator that said NO PETS ALLOWED. Every day they would look at that sign as they waited at the elevator. They hated that sign so much because they *loved* animals. They had hundreds of books and magazines about animals. They had pictures of giraffes, monkeys, penguins, and kittens on the walls of their bedrooms. It made their mother sad to know that her children couldn't have any animals of their own.

One day the mother came home from work with exciting news. As she stood by the elevator and read that awful sign she just smiled. "Children, come quick. I have wonderful news! We are moving! We are moving out of this city, across the river, and into the mountains, and you can have a *pet*!" _____ and _____ jumped up and down. They hugged each other and they hugged their mom with the biggest hug they had ever given her.

Soon the family packed their belongings into a moving van and traveled across the country. On the long trip the children tried to decide what kind of pet they would choose. It was very difficult because they loved all the animals. They arrived at their new home in the mountains and it was wonderful! There was a huge yard for a pet, but they just couldn't decide what animal to get.

One day the mother and the children took a walk through the forest to look at all the trees and plants and animals living there. It wasn't long before they became hopelessly lost. The more they tried to find their way out, the deeper into the forest they went. _____ and _____ started to cry. The mother tried to be brave, but she was frightened, too. Then from behind a tree came a soft roar. The three lost people held onto each other as the animal approached very, very carefully. The mountain lion appeared to be very gentle. Soon the lost family felt no fear as they softly stroked the lion's fur. Mother said, "Children, I believe we have just made a new friend. Let's call her Mali, Mali the Mountain

Lion." The children liked the name very much, but even though their fear of the forest was gone, they knew that they were still lost!

Soon, a very large owl flew down from the top of a tree. As _____ looked up in the tree, the owl looked down at her and softly said, "Whooo." Then the owl spread his huge wings and flew in a large circle over the heads of the lost hikers. He quietly flew back to the tree and again said, "Whooo." _____ said to her family, "I think the owl—let's call him Orlando—can show us how to get home if we watch him fly." They all agreed it just might work and as Orlando the Owl glided away, the little family followed. As they all struggled to keep their eyes on the owl, they would occasionally trip or bump into a tree. It was very difficult to look in the sky and not get hurt on the ground.

All of a sudden the biggest, blackest, curliest dog they had ever seen came running up to them and licked them all over. That dog wagged his tail and jumped all around. What a wonderful dog he was! He almost looked like he was smiling. _____ said to his mom, "Do you think this dog could be called Charger? I always wanted a dog named Charger!" Mother thought it was a grand name for such a fine dog. Charger ran ahead of them, looked back, and barked. The family just watched him. He ran up to them, ran off again, stopped and barked. _____ said, "I think Charger wants us to follow him!" So the family all grabbed on to Charger's black, curly coat and off they went.

Soon they came to the edge of the forest and saw their wonderful home. Waiting for them was Mali the _____ _____ and Orlando the _____. The children whispered in their mother's ear and she said, "What a wonderful idea! Friends, my children would like for you to be part of our family. We will give you food and water and a place to sleep. You will keep your freedom, but you will always know that we will be here for you and that we love you."

Everyone was very happy, and the children had made the wisest choice of all.

ACTIVITY 1

Draw an Animal

Materials

animals from the One-Week Zoo
Discovery Journals

The world is filled with an incredible diversity of life. Literally thousands of unique animals live in it. Although it is true that in their lifetime children will not see all of the different types of animals, they can come to understand that many unique animals live right in their immediate world.

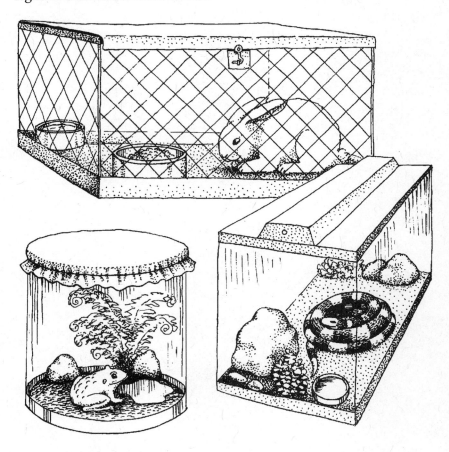

C•O•N•N•E•C•T•I•O•N•S

To Language

Expressive Language - Children will listen to one another as they share their drawings.

Discovery Journals - Children will tell you about their drawings as you write the dictated description.

What to Do

1. Allow time for each child to make a drawing of one of the animals in the One-Week Zoo in his or her Discovery Journal.

2. Say to each child: Tell me about your picture. The child should describe in detail the observations that have been made. Write down the descriptive information on the margin of the picture. Then ask the child to draw another animal and give information to you without your questioning. Record the free flow of information as it is expressed.

3. From time to time throughout the Animals unit, encourage children to repeat this activity.

4. When the children complete the Checkpoint activity, Draw an Animal Again (page 156), remember to refer to these initial drawings.

Science Concept

Animals display physical and behavioral diversity.

Science Process Skill

To focus observations by using the senses.

Science Vocabulary

animal names
animal traits, such as fur and feathers
different
diverse
unique

Assessing the Activity

The drawing and the detail given in the oral exchange about the drawing will be an indication of the child's observations and awareness of physical characteristics of various animals.

ACTIVITY 2

Touching Animals

Materials

animals from the One-Week Zoo
large sheet of newsprint

Touching animals can play an important role in the development of humane attitudes and scientific sensory skills. Handling animals allows children to use their tactile sense in ways that involve gross and fine motor skills. A shy child reaching out to feel the texture of a snake skin is introduced to a whole new sensory dimension. Cuddling a guinea pig draws the animal to the child in a nurturing manner.

Before the Activity

Tell the children which animals can be touched. Include cautions and special handling instructions as needed. Some animals may be handled only in the presence of an adult. A new rabbit might be best introduced quietly during group time.

What to Do

1. Talk about the sense of touch with the children. Brainstorm words that we use to describe the way things feel to us. This will generate a list of "feely" words, such as *soft, fuzzy, prickly,* and *slick*. Record these words on a Discovery Chart.

2. In groups of two or four, have the children select an animal. Very gently, so that the animal will not be hurt, let the children feel it. Ask: How does it feel?

C ▪ O ▪ N ▪ N ▪ E ▪ C ▪ T ▪ I ▪ O ▪ N ▪ S

To Language

Expressive Language - Children will develop vocabulary of descriptive words as they search for ways to describe what they feel and listen to each other's ideas.

Discovery Journals - Encourage the children to share their drawings with each other.

Science Concept

Animals display physical and behavioral diversity.

Science Process Skill

To focus observations by using the senses.

Science Vocabulary

animal characteristics, such as soft, smooth, and hairy, observed by using the sense of touch
animal names
tactile

3. Write additional words generated by the children on the chart in a different color. Compare these "feely" words to the words listed during the initial brainstorming activity.

4. Ask each child to make a drawing in their Discovery Journal of an animal he or she likes to touch.

Assessing the Activity

Look for refinement and greater detail in the children's comments than those brainstormed at the beginning of the activity.

ACTIVITY 3

How Does That Animal Move?

Materials

animals from the One-Week Zoo

Discovery Journals

The ways in which animals move are easy to observe but not easy to record. However, the children can observe and compare the movement of various animals, and then communicate these observations by role-playing the animal movements.

C·O·N·N·E·C·T·I·O·N·S

To Language

Expressive Language - Children will use descriptive language as they talk about the ways animals move. Role play gives them the opportunity to understand animals in a new way.

Discovery Journals - Children will record the movements of their favorite animals.

Science Concept

Animals display physical and behavioral diversity.

Science Process Skill

To focus observations by using the senses.

Science Vocabulary

animal names
change
movement
position

What to Do

1. Help the children focus their observations on one or more of the classroom animals as the animals move. Ask the children to describe the various movements.

2. Suggest that children demonstrate the movement of the different animals.

3. With the children, discuss why animals move the way they do. For example, ask: Why can't turtles jump like rabbits?

4. You may want to have the children add drawings to their Discovery Journals of their favorite animal moving.

Assessing the Activity

Observe the child's ability to demonstrate an awareness of the differences in various types of animal movement.

ACTIVITY 4

How Heavy Is It?

Materials

books and buckets (optional; see Before the Activity)

double-pan balance

animals from the One-Week Zoo

How Heavy Is It? sheet (see page 138)

paste

Discovery Journals

This activity asks the children to use the balance to make simple comparisons of mass (rather than actual measurements). By making multiple comparisons with many animals, children reinforce their understanding of rank ordering of objects from light to heavy. For this activity, the distinction between mass and weight is not critical as they are proportionate to one another.)

Before the Activity

If you have animals that are too big for the bowl of the balance, use small buckets to hold the animals. You will need an identical container on each side of the balance. If you wish to vary the activity's conclusion, you may want to have the children rank-order the animals from heaviest to lightest.

Ask the children for examples of things they consider heavy or light. If they do not seem to have a clear understanding, give them some examples. You can put five paperback books into one bucket and one large hardcover book into another bucket. Have a child lift them, one bucket in each hand. Ask: Which is heavy? Which is light? Use several examples until you feel that the concept is understood.

C▪O▪N▪N▪E▪C▪T▪I▪O▪N▪S

To Language

Expressive Language - The children are being asked to use comparative terms, this time *heavy* to *light*.

Discovery Journals - Let the children share their drawings and talk with each other about them.

To Math

Measuring and Estimating - Children will estimate which of two animals is heavier and then compare the animals by using the balance.

What to Do

1. Review the use of the balance with the children. Discuss the terms *heavy* and *light*. Ask the children to estimate which animals will be heavier and which will be lighter.

2. Select two animals to compare. Ask the children to guess which one is the heavier. Either the you or one of the children should place the two animals on the balance pans. Compare with the children which animal weighs more.

3. Select two more animals and make the same comparison. This comparison process may be repeated with all combinations of animals.

4. Have children draw pictures of a balance in their Discovery Journals with a heavy animal drawn on the low side of the balance and a light animal on the high side. Children might require some assistance in drawing a properly tilted balance. Squares from the How Heavy Is It? sheet may be pasted in Discovery Journals to show the action of the balance. Let the children share their drawings with each other.

Assessing the Activity

Review the Discovery Journal drawings. Do they reflect accurate comparisons of the animals?

ACTIVITY 5

I Am An Animal Too!

Materials

large sheets of newsprint (1 per child)
crayons
animals and/or animal pictures

This activity introduces children to the realization that they too are animals, with many of the same physical characteristics as the animals they are observing. The major emphasis of this activity is how humans are similar to and different from other types of animals. You will introduce a new type of animal, the "human being."

Before the Activity

Cut or tear enough sheets of paper for each child, large enough to trace around a child's entire body.

What to Do

1. Suggest that the children work in pairs to trace an outline of their bodies on the sheets of paper. Some children may need assistance.

2. Tell them to draw in facial features and fingers.

3. Have children compare their self-portraits to the other animals in the room or to pictures of animals. They should be looking for similarities and differences.

4. Have the class sit in a circle. Select a child and an animal and ask the child to tell what is alike and what is different between the child and the animal. For example, ask: Tomeka, look at this hamster. What do you have that this hamster has too? Another question might be asked of another child: Luis, what is different about you and this hamster?

C ▪ O ▪ N ▪ N ▪ E ▪ C ▪ T ▪ I ▪ O ▪ N ▪ S

To Language

Expressive Language - Children will actively verbalize thoughts about the similarities and differences they see as they compare themselves to other animals.

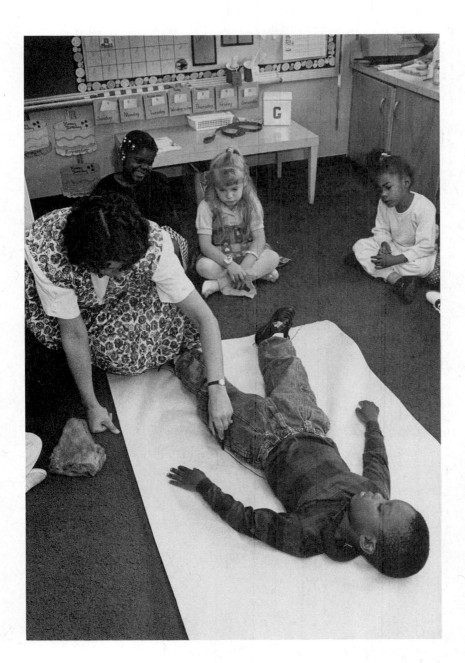

Science Concept

Animals display physical and behavioral diversity.

Science Process Skill

To focus observations by using the senses.

Science Vocabulary

alike
body parts such as eyes, ears, and fingers
different
human being
similar

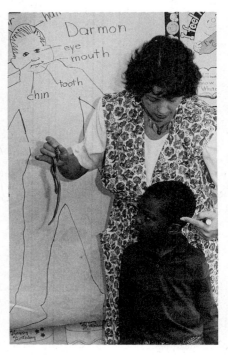

Assessing the Activity

How many accurate comparisons does each child make? Do they compare the features on their drawing with features of animals?

CHECKPOINT

Draw an Animal Again

Materials

animals from the One-Week Zoo
Discovery Journals

You will see significant development in children's attention to detail—a result of their experiences. Their drawings will become more accurate and detailed. The development of observation skills is what is important, not beautiful artwork.

What to Do

1. Ask the children to choose one of the animals in the Discovery Center and to draw that animal in their Discovery Journals. Have them caption the drawing at their own level of writing.

C•O•N•N•E•C•T•I•O•N•S

To Language

Expressive Language - Children will use terms to describe their animals in a story.

Discovery Journals - Children will caption their drawing at their level of writing ability.

2. Ask the children individually: Tell me about your picture. Offer the children opportunities to express themselves freely as they share their animal drawing from their Discovery Journals. Ask open-ended questions that support the expression of their own thoughts and feelings. Write descriptive information that a child gives you on the margin of the picture.

This is Erik. He is our class rabbit.

3. Encourage the children to compare this drawing with their first drawing.

Assessing the Activity

The drawing and the detail in the oral exchange about the drawing will be an indication of the child's observations and awareness of physical characteristics of various animals. Compare the drawing with the drawing produced in Activity 1, Draw an Animal (page 146).

Science Concept

Animals display physical and behavioral diversity.

Science Process Skill

To focus observations by using the senses.

Science Vocabulary

animal names
biped
descriptive words about animal traits, such as fur, feathers, size, skin, and claws
quadriped

ADDITIONAL STIMULATION

Play-Clay Creatures with Features

Materials

recipe for Play Clay
decorating materials, such as fur, yarn, toothpicks, buttons (option)

This activity provides a means to involve families. They will be working with the child to help the child create a clay animal. Be sure to stress that this is a child-directed activity in which family members are the assistants.

What to Do

1. Send home a letter to families explaining this family-child activity. Include the Play Clay recipe. Explain that the family is to help the child create an animal of the child's choice from the Play Clay. (Having the families and children make the Play Clay together is a valuable experience. However, if you think many families will not be able to comfortably provide the ingredients, you might want to make the Play Clay and send it home.)

2. You may want to provide, or have families provide, decorating materials—such as fur, yarn, toothpicks, and buttons—for the children to use to define their animals and to make them unique. In the letter, give the date when the animal constructions should be returned to school for the children to share and describe.

C·O·N·N·E·C·T·I·O·N·S

To Language

Expressive Language - A variety of language stimulation episodes are presented in this activity. Children and family members interact and make decisions as to what kind of animal to make. Discussion continues as the animal is constructed. Further language will occur as the animal is shared with family members and then with classmates.

To Math

Measuring - Children will practice basic measuring skills as they make Play Clay.

3. When the children bring their creations to school, create a special display for them. Have the children describe their creations, focusing on the physical characteristics of the animals they have created. Focusing on such things as skin covering or number of legs will develop observational skills as a foundation for later classification experiences. You may want to invite family members, or display and share the animals with other classes. Children may take their animals home after this activity.

Play Clay

Ingredients
250 ml (1 c.) flour
125 ml ($\frac{1}{2}$ c.) salt
30 ml (2 T.) vegetable oil
water added in small amounts to a
maximum 125 ml ($\frac{1}{2}$ c.) food coloring

Directions No cooking is required. Mix the water and the food coloring. Mix the flour and salt and pour the oil into the mixture. Add a small amount of colored water at a time until the clay has a smooth, workable consistency. Store in a plastic bag or airtight container.

Science Concept

Animals display physical and behavioral diversity.

Science Process Skill

To focus their observations using their senses.

Science Vocabulary

animal names
body covering names
body part names

Assessing the Activity

Observe the finished animals and children's descriptions of them. Have they created animals with realistic forms and functions (for example, legs for walking and eyes for seeing)?

ACTIVITY 6

Animals and the Senses

Materials

animals
sense cards (see page 137)
food items

Animals observe their surroundings through their senses. If we watch very closely, we can actually observe them using their sensory organs to make observations.

Before the Activity

Select an appropriate animal for this activity, one that will be easy to manage and obvious in its behavior. A small mammal such as a guinea pig or a rabbit would work nicely.

C ▪ O ▪ N ▪ N ▪ E ▪ C ▪ T ▪ I ▪ O ▪ N ▪ S

To Language

Expressive Language - Children will discuss the interesting observations they make as they watch the animals smelling, listening, and using their other sense organs. (They have probably never focused on animals in the act of observing. You might find out something you did not know about animals and get caught up in the conversation. Encourage the children to listen to each other's unique descriptions.)

What to Do

1. Show the children the sense cards. Ask them what sense each symbol stands for. Explain, for example, that the nose card means to watch the animal's nose and to observe what it is smelling.

2. Ask: Can your nose smell the same things as this animal's nose can? Put a piece of food in front of the animal. Ask: Does the animal smell it? You may want the children to smell the food too.

3. Go on to the other senses: sight, touch, hearing, and taste. Use the sense cards to designate on which sense the group is to focus. You may want to point out that although we can watch the animal eat, we cannot tell about its tasting.

4. Discuss with the children how the animal uses each of its senses to observe the world and how we use our senses in much the same manner.

5. Look at the variety of ways that the animal used each sense. Discuss how the children used their senses to observe the animal's actions. The sense of sight may have been the major focus, but other senses will have been used.

6. Send home Animals Family Connection Activity 1 (page 289).

Assessing the Activity

Children's discussion will indicate whether they have made meaningful observations.

Science Concept

Animals are living organisms that breathe, move, grow, and require nourishment.

Science Process Skill

To focus observations by using the senses.

Science Vocabulary

observation
observe
senses
sensory organ names

ACTIVITY 7

What Does Your Animal Eat?

Materials

selections of animals from the class collection

plates or trays

food selections

Each animal in your classroom collection will eat certain foods. In this activity the children are asked to observe each animal as it eats the food recommended for it and determine whether the animal will eat other foods. Does a mealworm eat bananas? They will have to find out.

Before the Activity

Select animals that will eat a wide variety of foods and that the children can watch easily. Cut up the food into appropriate sizes.

What to Do

1. As a class, encourage the children to discuss the foods they eat. Ask: What do you eat? What can't you eat? Begin a discussion with the children about their observations of animals and how the animals each eat particular foods. Ask: Do you think animals eat any of the same foods you do?

2. Have each group of children gather around a particular animal. Ask: What food does your animal eat the most of? Have the children watch the animal eat that food. (For example, they may watch a hamster eat its prepared hamster food.) Have the children share their observations concerning the animal's eating habits.

C • O • N • N • E • C • T • I • O • N • S

To Language

Expressive Language - Children will talk with each other about their observations and ideas for foods to try.

Science Concept

Animals are living organisms that breathe, move, grow, and require nourishment.

Science Process Skill

To focus observations by using the senses.

Science Vocabulary

consume
diet
eating habits
food items
nourishment
similar

3. Help the children select new foods from those available and prepare them for the animals.

4. Place the new food in with the animal. Ask the children to observe whether the animal eats the new food or its regular food.

5. Go through the entire set of foods that the children have chosen to test. You may want to limit this number to five or six.

6. Invite the children to determine which foods the animals will eat by eliminating the foods that the animal does not choose.

Assessing the Activity

Give each child an opportunity to recall the chosen or appropriate food type for a specific animal. (Some children will have demonstrated their ability to do this during the activity and will not need to be quizzed again.)

ACTIVITY 8

How Does Your Animal Drink?

Materials

selections of animals from the class collection

cups of water (1 per child)

Most animals cannot survive without a constant supply of water. Some animals, however, do not drink. Mealworms, for example, take water from the food they eat, so do better if they have a wet food source, such as a potato. In this activity the children will be asked to determine how each of the animals in the collection obtains water.

Before the Activity

Provide as much variety for the children as you can, from an obvious drinker, such as the guinea pig, to the mealworm, which takes water from its food. You will need to determine in advance the drinking habits of your animals. One way to have them drink on demand is to remove water from their cages the day before the lesson. Otherwise, the animals might not drink right away and the lesson will take some time.

C•O•N•N•E•C•T•I•O•N•S

To Language

Expressive Language - Children will share information about pets they have at home or other animals they have seen. Encourage the children to be original in their use of descriptive language.

Science Concept

Animals are living organisms that breathe, move, grow, and require nourishment.

Science Process Skill

To focus observations by using the senses.

Vocabulary

dehydrate
drink
food
intake
moisture
wet

What to Do

1. Give each child a cup of water or take the class to a drinking fountain for a drink. Talk with them about the fact that our bodies need water to be healthy. Ask: How do people drink?

2. Begin a discussion with the children about animals drinking. Discuss their observations of how animals take in water.

3. Instruct the children to observe each of the animals in the class and to determine how each drinks.

4. Ask the children to group drinking styles. Ask: Do the animals swallow like people, do they lick like cats, do they suck like butterflies, or do they get water from food and do not look like they are drinking at all?

Assessing the Activity

Talk with the children about what they did to find out how animals take in water. Does their discussion include some specific references to particular animals and how they drink?

ACTIVITY 9

How Does Your Animal Breathe?

Materials

selections of animals from the class collection

large sheet of newsprint

All animals have a basic need to breathe. Children will be familiar with the type of breathing they do and will recognize similar breathing in other animals. They may not be able to recognize other forms of breathing. For example, insects and spiders breath through spiracles (holes in the abdomen). Fish, tadpoles, and many other animals take oxygen from the water in their gills. This lesson will introduce the children to the concept of breathing and its necessity in all animals.

Before the Activity

You will need to determine the breathing habits of your animal selections. Provide as much variety as you can from the obvious breather that breathes through lungs, such as the guinea pig or rabbit; to the mealworm and other insects; to fish, which breath through gills.

What to Do

1. Talk with the children about their observations of animals breathing. Ask whether they have ever seen a dog pant. Use human breathing as a model, and talk about some of the class's observations of the larger animals.

C ▪ O ▪ N ▪ N ▪ E ▪ C ▪ T ▪ I ▪ O ▪ N ▪ S

To Language

Expressive Language - Children will use both recall and direct observation as they talk about the breathing of animals in the classroom and animals they have seen at other times. Encourage them to use terms such as *fast* and *slow* as they compare breathing rates.

2. Ask the children to observe the animals and to determine whether each is breathing. Ask: Is this animal breathing fast or slow? Some animals breath very fast, and the children will not be about to count the inhalations; in this case, a comparison to their own breathing would be appropriate. Record their observations on a Discovery Chart.

3. When each of the animals has been observed, ask the children to group breathing styles. Ask: Do they breath like people? Can you see any breathing at all? Do they breath under water like a fish? Do all animals with a nose breathe in the same way?

Assessing the Activity

Have the children describe the breathing of an individual animal and how they are able to determine this.

Science Concept

Animals are living organisms that breathe, move, grow, and require nourishment.

Science Process Skill

To focus observations by using the senses.

Science Vocabulary

breathing
exhale
inhale
rapid
respiration

How Does Your Animal Breathe?	
animal	?
fish	can't see maybe gills on neck
guinea pig	nose
mouse	nose
earth worm	can't see Dad says through skin

ACTIVITY 10

How Does Your Animal Move?

Materials

animals from the class collection

Discovery Journals

A wildlife expert can find animals in the forest because of the predictability of their movement. This predictability is also evident in the animals in your classroom. Many of them have a movement that can be recorded and understood. Even for human beings, movement is often predictable. Children usually come into school through the same door, because that is where the bus drops them off. This activity will help them discover whether any of the classroom animals have predictable patterns.

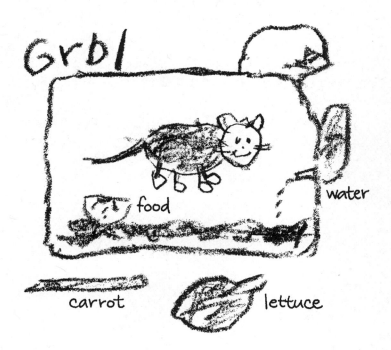

C▪O▪N▪N▪E▪C▪T▪I▪O▪N▪S

To Language

Expressive Language - This activity provides a good opportunity to use position words. The children will talk about the hamster going *around* in its wheel; the gerbil sleeping *in* its house; the turtle coming *in* and *out* of its shell; and the lizard climbing *up* and *down* the branch.

Science Concept

Animals are living organisms that breathe, move, grow, and require nourishment.

Science Process Skill

To focus observations by using the senses.

Science Vocabulary

movement
movement words
pattern
predictable

What to Do

1. Choose an animal with a predictable movement pattern. This might be a hamster that regularly runs on a wheel, a goldfish that swims in circles, or a gerbil that sleeps most of the day.

2. Ask the children to describe what the selected animal usually does.

3. Ask the children to observe the classroom animals over the next several days. Have them make observations of the movement of each animal and record their observations in their Discovery Journals.

Assessing the Activity

Have the child describe movement patterns for one of the animals.

CHECKPOINT

Is It Alive? Tell Us Why

Materials

animals from the class collection

nonliving objects, such as rocks, bones, animal toys, dolls, mechanical toys, and pieces of plastic

2 pages of newsprint

The concept of living and nonliving is an important one for the young child. We describe a living thing as something that breathes, moves, grows, and requires nourishment. This activity will focus children's observations on each of these aspects.

Before the Activity

Decide which animals you will use for the living objects. Prepare a Discovery Chart by writing the headings Living and Nonliving at the top.

What to Do

1. Show the children an animal and a nonliving object.

2. After the children have had time to observe, ask them to identify the characteristics of each of the two objects. Ask: What differences do you see? In what ways are the objects the same? Which object is not alive? How do you know which is alive and which is not alive? Record their responses on the Discovery Chart.

3. Repeat the process several times to include a variety of animals and objects. Your selections can guide the children in developing more complete understanding of living and non-

C ■ O ■ N ■ N ■ E ■ C ■ T ■ I ■ O ■ N ■ S

To Language

Expressive Language - You may want to make Venn diagrams with the children.

To Math

Comparing - The children will make direct comparisons of movement, size, and temperature.

Science Concepts

Animals are living organisms that breathe, move, grow, and require nourishment.

Science Process Skill

To focus observations by using the senses.

Science Vocabulary

animal names
characteristic
living
nonliving

living	nonliving
guinea pig	teddy bear
• has fur	• has fur
• moves	• does not move
• has two eyes	• has two eyes
• eats	• does not eat
• wrinkles its nose	• does not move its nose
• feels warm	• does not feel warm
• feel it breathing	• cannot feel it breathing
• tries to get away	• stays in same place
• makes noises	• never makes noise

living things. For example, if a child says the guinea pig is alive because it has hair, include a doll with hair in the next pair. A child may say a worm is alive because it moves. Show a wind-up toy next. Notice, for example, how they describe the living and nonliving characteristics of a live rabbit and a stuffed one.

4. You may want to make a Venn diagram with the children. Draw two overlapping circles on a page of newsprint and label them Living and Nonliving. The intersection is for nonliving objects that were once part of living organisms.

Assessing the Activity

Have each child come to the Discovery Chart and state one characteristic of living things and one characteristic of nonliving things. Work with small groups to get several responses from each child.

ACTIVITY 11

Where Animals Live: Wet or Dry?

Materials

one or more of the following animals (no mammals): earthworm, sow bug, mealworm, snail

appropriate habitat components, such as dirt, leaves, and bran flakes

water

pan (1 per type of animal)

large sheet of newsprint

paper towels

Discovery Journals

Each animal lives in a particular type of habitat. In this activity you will place animals in an environment with both a wet and a dry location. Each animal will either move to a specific place or remain scattered throughout the area. If you use more than one type of animal in this investigation, you can compare the different animals.

Before the Activity

Select several of each type of animal. Each species will be tested separately. Prepare a Wet/Dry Discovery Chart by writing the headings Wet and Dry at the top of the sheet of newsprint and the names of the animals down the side.

C▪O▪N▪N▪E▪C▪T▪I▪O▪N▪S

To Language

Expressive Language - Children will share with each other the variety of habitats that animals live in and classify animals by their reactions to different kinds of environments. (You might ask the children: If you were outside, where would I look for you? This is a good time to introduce habitat terms that are specific to the animal, such as *moist, dry, damp, wet, desert,* and *swampy*. Many excellent books are available for young children on the subject of animal habitats.)

Discovery Journals - Children will share their drawings, which match animals to habitats. Support their creative attempts at "mapping" the locations of the animals.

To Math

Counting, Charting, and Comparing - Children will count the number of animals selecting the wet environment and those selecting the dry environment, record these observations in a chart, and make a comparison between the habitat reactions of different animals.

What to Do

1. Prepare the habitat for the study (you may want the children to help). For mealworms place a layer of bran flakes in the pan; for earthworms use a 2- to 4-centimeter layer of dirt; and for snails and sow bugs use a clean pan with leaves on the bottom.

2. Place a wet, crumpled towel at one end of the pan and a dry one at the other end. The investigation may be made even more complex by placing a dripping wet, a moist, and a dry towel in the location. (The focus is to provide a moist environment for the animals, not drown them!) Place the animals of one kind into the center of the pan.

3. Have the children observe the habitat and the location of the animals. Some of the animals may be thirsty and will come to the wet towel for a drink. Discuss the difference between *living in* and *drinking* water. Careful observation and notation of position will allow the children to see how the animals in the pans are moving. This movement is not always obvious because an individual is only seen in its current location.

4. On the next day, locate the animals. If the animals take several days to move, add water to the towel to keep it wet.

5. Ask the children to note carefully the animals' locations. Have the children draw in their Discovery Journals where each animal is found.

6. Have children count the animals on the wet side and on the dry side. Record this on the Wet/Dry chart.

7. You may want to use other animals in a second investigation to make a comparison.

Assessing the Activity

Both the children's drawings and entries they suggest for addition to the Discovery Chart may be used to determine whether children are clearly observing what is taking place.

Science Concept

Animals interact with their environment.

Science Process Skill

To focus observations by using the senses.

Science Vocabulary

adapt
compare
environment
habitat
location
respond

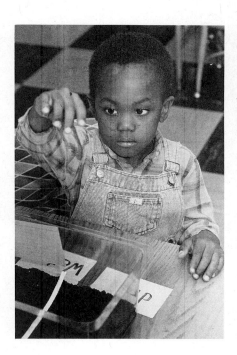

ACTIVITY 12

Hiding Out

Materials

selections of animals from the class collection
sheets of dark paper
boxes and lids
light sources
Discovery Journals

This activity draws the children's attention to another reaction seen in animals. Each animal has specific light and dark needs. Animals such as crickets, mealworms, pill bugs, and to some degree, mice and hamsters, will spend much of the daytime in a dark place.

What to Do

1. Begin a discussion with the children about their observations of animals and how some animals will hide or stay under things in their cages. Explain that this behavior might be an animal's reaction to light; some animals spend most of their time in dark places, and some spend time in the light. Ask: Where does a cat stay? A dog? A hamster? Why might an animal spend time in dark places? Say: Let's find out if our animals spend time in the light or the dark.

2. Show the children how to position light sources so they will illuminate the cages or pans but not get them too hot.

C▪O▪N▪N▪E▪C▪T▪I▪O▪N▪S

To Language

Expressive Language - Children will share with each other their observations about the variety of habitats in which animals live. (Urge the children to share their independent observations. You may want to have picture books on nocturnal animals available for the children to use.)

Discovery Journals - Many animals are investigated in this activity. Encourage the children to use inventive writing to describe the two animals "hiding out" as they draw.

Science Concept

Animals interact with their environment.

Science Process Skill

To focus observations by using the senses.

Science Vocabulary

dark
diurnal
light
nocturnal
reaction
respond

3. Discuss with the children the things they discovered in Activity 10, How Does Your Animal Move? The children's recollection of this information will get them interested in how animals will respond to light and dark.

4. Have the children choose the animals they wish to observe. Give them dark paper, a box, or box lids to place in the cages to create darkened areas. For a mealworm, place the paper on one area of the pan, leaving half of the pan exposed to light. For a hamster or gerbil, supply a small box. Let the children figure out how to create light and dark spaces.

5. Give the animals time to react to the light. Some animals will relocate quickly; others, like the mealworm, will take all night. Ask the children to note changes in location.

6. Have the children draw pictures in their Discovery Journals of one animal that stays in the light and one that moves to the dark.

Assessing the Activity

Can the children identify which animal will move to a light or a dark location when given that option? Do they indicate that their prediction of the animal's reaction is based on their observations?

CHECKPOINT

What Do We Know About Our Animals?

Material

crayons
Discovery Journals

Animals have needs for specific foods and habitats. In the wild these requirements are more pronounced and help scientists define an animals' behavior and territorial range. The hamster originated in the deserts of the Far East, and children should see from their investigation that it lives in dry places. Years of living in captivity have changed the hamster's food habits, but this is not in the scope of the children's research. They will have seen, though, that the hamster selects certain foods and habitat.

What to Do

1. Have the children draw an animal of their choice in their Discovery Journals.

2. Now have them draw pictures of the things they know about this animal. Tell them to include where the animal lives, the foods it eats, whether it tends to move toward light or dark, its response to odors, and any other information. Tell them to surround their animal pictures with these drawings. Encourage

C▪O▪N▪N▪E▪C▪T▪I▪O▪N▪S

To Language

Expressive Language - By now the children should be comfortable using many of the science vocabulary words introduced in the Animals unit. As they talk with you and among themselves, note this expanded vocabulary.

Discovery Journals - Children will review their earlier Discovery Journal entries just as a scientist doing research would do.

Written Language - Children will use their writing skills, at whatever level, to label their drawings.

children to write as many labels for their drawings as they can at their own level of literacy. Have them review past Discovery Journal pages for information on their animals.

Snake

This animal likes Watr AnD likes Frogs.

Watr

3. Ask the children to share their drawings and their conclusions regarding animal needs.

Assessing the Activity

The drawings should indicate that the children have made significant observations regarding animal environments. The children's conversations will also indicate their level of learning. This is a good time to review Discovery Charts created in the previous activities. This review not only reinforces the concepts but also communicates the function of written language.

Science Concept

Animals interact with their environment.

Science Process Skill

To focus observations by using the senses.

Science Vocabulary

animal names
climate names
environment
food names
habitat names
interact

ACTIVITY 13

Everything Has a Life Cycle

Materials

butterfly kit with growing chambers
magnifiers
interlocking cubes
daily Discovery Chart
Discovery Journals

The butterfly is well enough known to most children that you can use it to demonstrate the concept of life cycle. You and the class will watch the butterfly's development and document it in detail. This activity takes almost a month to complete.

Before the Activity

Order a Painted Lady butterfly kit from a science supply house several weeks in advance. Live eggs are not included; instead, you will find a mailer with which to order eggs. (Many suppliers will not mail during cold weather.) When you receive the butterfly media and growing chamber, prepare them according to the directions. You may want to prepare new Discovery Journals for the butterfly watching.

What to Do

1. Tell the children that they will be watching the eggs develop into butterflies and will record that development in detail. The changes that will occur in the organisms will be much different from changes in other organisms, such as humans.

C▪O▪N▪N▪E▪C▪T▪I▪O▪N▪S

To Language

Expressive Language - Children will develop oral communication skills. You may want to take photographs throughout the butterfly life cycle and put them on a poster with the children's captions.

Discovery Journals - Children will draw the changes they observe in the butterflies.

To Math

Counting and Measuring - Children will count animals and measure their growth.

The changes are slow, and you may have to remind the children to make their observations. Over the weeks a larva (caterpillar) will hatch from each egg, grow, develop into a pupa (chrysalis), and then into a Painted Lady butterfly. You will probably need to make drawings only when these significant steps occur. Note day 1 on the Discovery Chart.

2. Discuss with the children that all baby animals go through a set of changes as they grow into adults. Talk about their own life cycle and the life cycles of animals they have observed.

3. The butterflies will move through their life cycle slowly but predictably. Direct the children to make periodic observations to discover and confirm that fact. Have them draw the butterflies in their Discovery Journals as they observe changes taking place. Suggest that they note the location of the animals, the animal's movements, and their eating habits. Remind them to record the dates that observations are made. Have them keep track of how many of the larvae hatch, how many develop into a pupa, and how many become butterflies.

4. Hold periodic discussions to corroborate these observations. Demonstrate how to measure growth of the larvae; for example, with interlocking cubes. You may want to ask the children to draw their own human life cycle.

5. End the study with a summary and ask the class to help develop a full-size drawing of the butterfly life cycle.

Assessing the Activity

The drawings should show both physical and behavioral observations. Given one of their drawings, the children should be able to describe physical and behavioral characteristics.

Science Concept

Animals grow and change throughout their lives.

Science Process Skill

To focus observations by using the senses.

Science Vocabulary

adult
butterfly
change
develop
egg
grow
growth
life cycle

CHECKPOINT

The Human Life Cycle

Materials

paper

glue or paste

scissors

magazines with pictures of people of all ages

photographs the children bring from home (optional)

newsprint (optional)

Every living organism has a life cycle. Some are simple, some are complex, some may take only a few weeks, and others one hundred years or more; the human life cycle is one of the longest. Always, however, a life cycle is predictable and replicable. An animal usually begins as an egg, moves through a stage marked by rapid growth, a juvenile or maturing stage, and finally grows into an adult. The adult stage—including reproduction, aging, and death—is usually the longest part of the life cycle.

This activity gives children an opportunity to talk about similarities and differences in life cycles of some of the animals they have studied and to share information about their own families. This sharing can be interesting, as it is often at this age that children begin to grapple with ideas such as the fact that a person can be their mother and their grandmother's daughter at the same time. This realization is amazing to many young children.

Before the Activity

The children will be making a life-cycle book. Make your normal preparations for a slightly messy project. Cut out one picture each of a baby, a child, a teenager, an adult, and an elderly adult for your introduction.

C▪O▪N▪N▪E▪C▪T▪I▪O▪N▪S

To Language

Expressive Language - Children will share experiences they have had with life cycles.

Written Language - Children will use their own level of writing ability to caption their books.

What to Do

1. Review with the children the experience of watching the Painted Lady butterflies grow and develop. Talk again about how people change throughout their lives. Ask the children to talk about the people they know at various stages in the human life cycle. Display the four pictures. Ask: Which picture do you think should come first? Next?

2. Tell the children that they are each going to make a life-cycle book. Each book will have a page for each stage of the human life cycle. Tell them to cut out one or more pictures for each stage of human development. Distribute the magazines and let the children cut out pictures.

3. Distribute the paper and glue. Have the children glue pictures onto the pages. Move among them and help as needed.

4. Allow each child to make a collage or a drawing for a book cover.

5. One extension of this activity would be to make a bulletin-board collage of photographs that you and the children bring in to illustrate the stages of the human life cycle. If the children need more work on life cycles, suggest that they create more collages or books on the life cycles of other animals.

Assessing the Activity

Did the knowledge the children gained from watching the butter-flies in the previous activity appear to transfer as you began to discuss the human life cycle? Listen to the children as they work. How do they describe the various stages of human growth and development? Ask them about the pictures they selected. Do the children exhibit an understanding of the concept of growth and change over time?

Science Concept

Animals grow and change throughout their lives.

Science Process Skill

To focus observation by using the senses.

Science Vocabulary

adult
aging
change
infant
juvenile
life cycle
predictable
reproduction
teenager

ACTIVITY 1

Who's Who? Classifying Animal Pictures

Materials

magazines containing photographs of animals

pictures and photographs of animals clipped from magazines

photographs of pets (brought from home)

1 shoe box (per child or group)

scissors

glue or paste

paper

The greater the variety of animals the children experience, the better the scientific observations they can make. Some ways to create this diversity beyond actual hands-on experience are to have the children see films or videos, visit the zoo, or look at pictures or photographs of animals. In this activity the children will explore animals through photographs.

Before the Activity

Begin your collection of animal pictures early, and include photographs of animals brought into the classroom and of children's pets. Decide whether children are to cut out pictures in class before the activity or whether you or family volunteers will provide cut-out pictures. If children will be doing the cutting, allow a few days to make the picture collections.

C·O·N·N·E·C·T·I·O·N·S

To Language

Expressive Language - Children will verbalize as they cut out pictures and make animal photograph collections. They will talk about physical likenesses or differences and observable behavioral characteristics.

To Math

Counting and Grouping - Children will count and group the number of animals that fall into a specific grouping; for example, How many animals have scales?

What to Do

1. Give a child or group of children a shoe box filled with pictures of animals.

2. Instruct the children to classify the pictures by placing them into groupings they choose themselves, such as color, shape, size, legs, external covering (hair, scales, feathers), movement (walk, crawl, fly, swim), habitat (ground, trees, water), wild or tame, edible or not, or what they eat.

3. Encourage the children to try different groupings as they repeat this activity. Accept their groupings as they offer their explanations and reasoning. Have them count the number in each group.

4. Have each group create an animal collage using only one attribute, such as animals having hair.

Assessing the Activity

A reasonable observation or rationale for grouping the animals is adequate evaluation.

Science Concept

Animals display physical and behavioral diversity.

Science Process Skill

To use observations to classify.

Science Vocabulary

characteristics
classify
group
grouping names, such as body covering, habitat, and movement
sort

ACTIVITY 2

Alike and Different

Materials (per group)

sets of picture cards of the classroom animals

five cards with *alike* written on them and five cards with *different* (you may want to use visual cues in addition to the words)

When children explore similarities and differences among animals, they begin to realize that the same animal may be a part of several groups. Although pictures cannot take the place of the real thing, they offer the opportunity to bring the diversity of the animal kingdom into the classroom. In this activity you use picture cards for a game, but encourage the children to return to the live animals for actual observations or to check an observation.

Before the Activity

Create sets of picture cards of the classroom animals. For each set, make one card for each animal living in or visiting your classroom. You may make cards from photographs, pictures, drawings, or the children's drawings. Under each picture write the name of the animal.

What to Do

1. Explain to the children that they are to mix the picture cards and spread them out face down. Then they are to mix the Alike and Different cards and turn them upside down in a stack.

C ▪ O ▪ N ▪ N ▪ E ▪ C ▪ T ▪ I ▪ O ▪ N ▪ S

To Language

Expressive Language - The game requires the children to draw conclusions about similarities and differences, an important skill in emerging literacy.

Written Language - Children will discriminate between the printed words *alike* and *different*.

To Math

Counting- You might have children count the number of animals that fall into a specific group.

Science Concept

Animals display physical and behavioral diversity.

Science Process Skill

To use observations to classify objects into groups.

Science Vocabulary

alike
animal names
attribute
characteristics
different

2. Explain that the first player is to choose two animal cards and one Alike or Different card. Then the player is to state a likeness or difference between the two animals. If, for example, white rat, guinea pig, and Alike are selected, a correct answer would be that both animals have hair. (You may suggest that one characteristic may be observed or as many as possible before selecting new cards.) The child returns the cards, and the second player takes a turn.

3. If this activity is done as a class, write the observations on the board. You might want children to practice their counting skills. For example, you could ask: How many animals have scales?

4. Send home Animals Family Connection Activity 2 (page 289).

Assessing the Activity

This activity provides the opportunity for you to assess the children's understanding of the terms *alike*, *different*, and *same*. Each child should be able to state one alike and one different characteristic for each pair of animals.

ACTIVITY 3

The Right Place to Live

Materials

animals from the class collection.
Discovery Charts (1 per child)
large sheets of newsprint
tape
crayons
Discovery Journals

Determining whether an animal would be appropriate as a pet where we live requires an understanding of both our environment and the animal. A child may love horses, for example, but could not keep one in an apartment. Guinea pigs or mealworms might be ideal pets in a small apartment, because they would fit and would make little noise. In this activity you ask the children to look at several animals and decide whether or not the animals could live in various environments.

Before the Activity

Prepare individual Discovery Charts for the children to tape into their Discovery Journals. Prepare a large summary Discovery Chart. See the example; other possible columns are a fenced-in backyard, a barn, and an aquarium.

C▪O▪N▪N▪E▪C▪T▪I▪O▪N▪S

To Language

Expressive Language - As the children group the animals, they will be looking for common characteristics. Encourage them to explain their decisions. Reinforce the idea that different animals are ideal for different situations and that all are necessary.

Discovery Journals - Children will prepare individual Discovery Charts for their Discovery Journals.

Written Language - Children will reinforce emerging writing skills by writing *yes* or *no* on individual charts.

To Math

Classifying and Charting - Children will classify each animal according to their opinion of the animal's suitability as a pet. Children will use a chart as a means of recording their perceptions and then compare these perceptions from animal to animal and with each other.

Animal	Your room	Pond	Large glass tank
1. Guinea pig	yes (or Y)	no (or N)	yes (or Y)
2. Mealworm			
3.			

What to Do

1. Hold up an animal and ask the children to mark on their Discovery Charts whether they could have the animal as a pet in the habitat named in the first column. Children may use a Y or N, or some another system (such as a smiling/frowning face). Then ask the same question for the other habitat columns.

2. Give the children the opportunity to look at several of the classroom animals and to record their opinions independently.

3. Bring the children back as a group, and ask them to share their results. Ask: How many looked at a guinea pig? What did you write down on your chart? What were your reasons? Discuss any disagreements. Record the information on a large Discovery Chart. Continue with the other animals.

4. Urge the children to draw pictures in their Discovery Journals of the animal they would like to have as a pet in their own home.

Science Concept

Animals display physical and behavioral diversity.

Science Process Skill

To use observations to classify objects into groups.

Science Vocabulary

chart
classify
habitat
record
select

Assessing the Activity

This activity begins classification theory with the concept of single-stage classification. Classification is built on observation, so identification of the reason or observational base for each grouping is important. Do the children use accurate criteria for classifying animals? Try asking the children how they can provide a good home for their chosen pet.

ACTIVITY 4

Shell Shadows

Materials

2 sets of shells of different shapes and sizes (for example, a set of snail shells of different sizes and a set of scallop shells of different sizes)

other shells of different shapes (optional)

overhead projector and screen

The natural variation in seashells, along with their beauty, makes them a focus of children's curiosity. They are natural objects that children can group in a variety of ways.

What to Do

1. Show the children some shells. Discuss how shells were once the protective homes of living animals. The shells washed up on the beach and were collected.

2. Place one shell from each set on the overhead projector so that the two shell *shapes* project onto a screen.

3. Tell the children that two different kinds of shells are projected on the screen. Make sure children notice the shells' different shapes. Place a third shell on the projector and ask the children to help sort the three shells into two shape groups. Continue adding shells and talking with the children, asking them in which group each additional shell shape belongs.

C ▪ O ▪ N ▪ N ▪ E ▪ C ▪ T ▪ I ▪ O ▪ N ▪ S

To Language

Expressive Language - Children will use scientific thinking and vocabulary as they work together to classify shells. They will state the reason they think a shell should be classified as part of a particular group.

To Math

Sorting, Classifying, and Comparing - Children will direct the sorting of shells into groups of similar characteristics, classify the shells according to two attributes, and compare characteristics when deciding to which group an additional shell belongs.

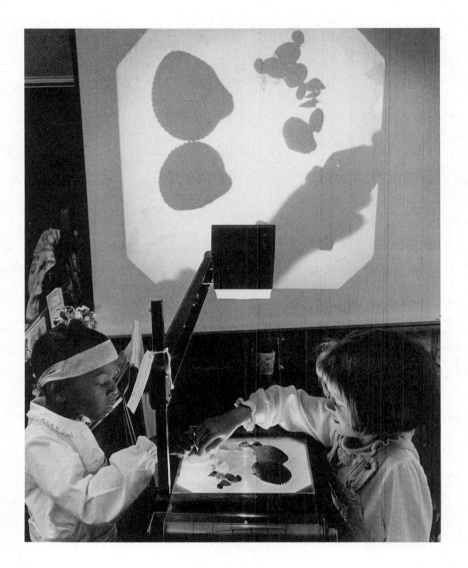

Science Concept

Animals display physical and behavioral diversity.

Science Process Skill

To use observations to classify objects.

Science Vocabulary

characteristics
classify
group
shadow
sort
symmetry

4. Repeat with the characteristic of *size*.

5. As an optional extension, introduce shells with shapes different from the two sets.

Assessing the Activity

Give a child a shell to be added to the groups on the overhead. Observe in which group the child places the shell and discuss with the child why he or she placed the shell in that group.

ACTIVITY 5

Classifying the Animal Discovery Collection

Materials

items from the Animal Discovery Collection

yarn

The Animal Discovery Collection provides children with a rich supply of different manipulatives and an unlimited variety of recognizable attributes. The real challenge for children in this classification activity is focusing on a single attribute that many of the objects have in common. With so much diversity and stimulation, achieving this focus is often difficult.

Before the Activity

Select items from the Animal Discovery Collection that lend themselves to classification. Make several yarn loops, using about a meter of yarn for each. Different colors of yarn can be helpful in differentiating categories.

C·O·N·N·E·C·T·I·O·N·S

To Language

Expressive Language - Children will discuss the various common attributes among the objects they group.

To Math

Counting and Classifying - Children will count objects as they sort them into groups according to similar attributes. (By making Venn diagram with circles of yarn, children clearly observe the separation and distinctions that are made between objects. Overlapping yarn circles can show that objects can share some properties but do not share all properties.)

Science Concept

Animals display physical and behavioral diversity.

Science Process Skill

To use observations to classify objects into groups.

Science Vocabulary

characteristics
classify
group
overlap
properties

What to Do

1. Hold up several unique objects from the Animal Discovery Collection. Call attention to some differences and similarities, and ask children which objects could be grouped together. Show them how to make circles from the yarn loops to use as boundaries for groups.

2. Encourage the children to classify the objects and to place them into the appropriate yarn circles. Have them count the number of objects placed in each group. Ask: Are some groups easier to form?

3. As the children become more familiar with the objects, they may see how objects can fit into two groups. Show them how to show this grouping can be shown by overlapping the yarn boundaries.

Assessing the Activity

Children should be able to identify and verbalize the properties they used to organize their objects into groups. They should also be able to explain why a particular object is or is not in a certain group.

CHECKPOINT

Pairs

Materials (per group)

sets of 10 or more shell pairs, some shell pairs of different sizes

Classification activities with shells expose the variety that exists naturally in the collection. This lesson introduces the concept that any collection of the same species will show a range of sizes. The children will be matching pairs that are of the same species, yet differ in size. They will soon be aware of the vast differences present in any shell collection.

Before the Activity

Prepare the shell collection, making sure matched pairs are available. The sets should have a variety of sizes for the pairs.

What to Do

1. Give each group of two or four children a set of shells.

2. Instruct them to classify the shells by matching the pairs. Explain what pair means by selecting one of the pair sets and matching it for the children. For example, say: The big and small scallop shells are a scallop shell pair.

C ▪ O ▪ N ▪ N ▪ E ▪ C ▪ T ▪ I ▪ O ▪ N ▪ S

To Language

Expressive Language - Children will verbalize the properties the various shell pairs have in common.

To Math

Comparing and Classifying - Children will compare the shells in a set as they look for possible shell pairs and place shells together as a set.

Science Concept

Animals display physical and behavioral diversity.

Science Process Skill

To use observations to classify objects.

Science Vocabulary

classify
characteristics
match
pairs
same

3. Explain that scientists who study animals classify things that are exactly the same except for size differences into the same groups.

4. Ask the children to explain the reason they placed a particular pair together.

Assessing the Activity

After the children have finished matching pairs, evaluate their effort. Ask why certain pairs were made. Ask for reasons, which should be based on one or more observable characteristics. Show a pair that the children have not seen and ask whether the two are a pair or not. Correct answers will indicate children's mastery of the concept of pairs.

Animal Odds and Ends

ADDITIONAL STIMULATION

Materials (per group)

10 to 12 items from the Animal Discovery Collection

1 shoe box or box lid

The Animal Discovery Collection can provide a myriad of classification activities. The greater the diversity in the objects you have collected, the more opportunities the children will have for additional stimulation.

Before the Activity

Prepare the shoe boxes, each containing 10 to 12 items from the Animal Discovery Collection.

What to Do

1. Divide the class into groups of two or four and give each group one of the prepared boxes.

2. Ask the groups to look at their collections. Have them place the objects into groups and explain their classification system.

3. Ask: Can you group the same objects another way?

4. Direct the groups to trade boxes and repeat the process. Urge them to find different ways to classify the collections.

5. Send home Animals Family Connection Activity 3 (page 289).

C ▪ O ▪ N ▪ N ▪ E ▪ C ▪ T ▪ I ▪ O ▪ N ▪ S

To Language

Expressive Language - Children will discuss attributes with each other and decide how to group objects. (Encourage the use of descriptive language.)

To Math

Comparing and Classifying - Children will select objects from the Animal Discovery Collection and devise appropriate classification systems for the objects selected.

Science Concept

Animals display physical and behavioral diversity.

Science Process Skill

To use observations to classify objects.

Science Vocabulary

classify
names of items in the collection
properties

Assessing the Activity

As you watch the children identify attributes and classify the collections, you will be able to assess their mastery of classification.

ACTIVITY 1

Measuring Animals

Materials

interlocking cubes
animals from the One-Week Zoo
2 large sheets of newsprint
construction paper (optional)
scissors (optional)
Discovery Journals

Measurement skills are as essential to the young learner as they are to the practicing scientist. Nonstandard measurement experiences will allow the children to compare the animals more precisely and help prepare the children for later work with the standard metric measurement of the scientist.

Before the Activity

Prepare a chart page and tape a copy in each student's journal. Choose the animals to be measured. The greater the variety of sizes, the easier it will be for the children to visualize the variation that exists in the animal world. You may want to do this over a week so that the animals are not exhausted from handling.

What to Do

1. Show the children how to measure the animals by using interlocking cubes.

2. Show the children how to use the animal chart page. The children will draw a picture of the animal in the first column. In the second column, they will record the animal's length by drawing the number of cubes used or by cutting squares from construction paper and gluing down the appropriate number.

C ■ O ■ N ■ N ■ E ■ C ■ T ■ I ■ O ■ N ■ S

To Language

Expressive Language - The children will probably be comfortable with the terms *big* and *little*. Use words such as *long, longest, tallest,* and *smallest* to add to their growing understanding of comparative language.

To Math

Measuring, Charting, and Graphing - Children will measure the animals, and help construct a chart and a graph of the measurements.

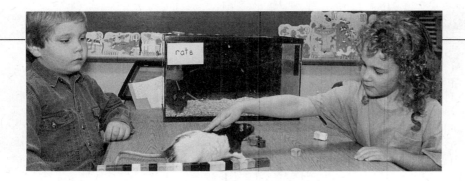

3. Have the children work in pairs to measure at least two animals. When all the children have completed the measurements, conduct a sharing session to compare the values. Ask: Are there differences in the measurements of the same animals? Talk with the children about possible reasons.

4. Make a class chart of all the animals measured. If a measurement of a particular animal is consistent, record the value. If a measurement is inconsistent, discuss the differences and measure again as a class.

5. Prepare a large bar graph of the results. Put the animal names along the horizontal axis and the measurements along the vertical axis. Ask: What does the bar graph show?

Assessing the Activity

Review the children's measurements during class discussion. Are their measurements reasonably accurate?

Science Concept

Animals display physical and behavioral diversity.

Science Process Skill

To focus observations by using the senses.

Science Vocabulary

compare
graph
measure
metric terms, such as centimeter and meter

Measuring Animals	
animal	length
box turtle	11
earth worm	9
rabbit	15
chinchilla	21
frog	3
snail	1
hamster	6
gerbil	9

ACTIVITY 2

Watching Animals Grow

Materials

growth chart

one or more baby animals, such as hamsters, gerbils, guinea pigs, mice, or kittens

double-pan balance

interlocking cubes

Discovery Journals

Growth is a basic characteristic of all living things. Animal growth in each species is a well-defined series of events. After birth, the individual grows rapidly. Plateaus, during which little growth takes place, are followed by periods of extremely rapid growth. At some point, growing stops. Almost all organisms have a maximum size. In this activity children follow the growth of an animal in a formalized way. This will probably take a few weeks, whether they are observing gerbils or puppies. Their observations, recorded in drawings and perhaps words, will capture the animals' changes.

Before the Activity

Prepare a growth chart, with one column for mass and one for length, that can be displayed on or near the animal's cage or dwelling. You will have to set rules about handling very young animals. Baby animals are fragile, and if they are handled, the mothers sometimes become agitated.

Your balance may not be accurate enough to assess the mass of tiny babies. If so, put them in the balance all at once and divide by the number of animals in the group.

C • O • N • N • E • C • T • I • O • N • S

To Language

Expressive Language - Children will talk about the changes animals go through as they mature. Their vocabulary should expand as they describe changes in appearance and size. This is a good time to observe the children's use of descriptive and comparative language.

To Math

Measuring - Children will measure both length and volume.

Guinea Pig Growth Chart	
time	length
day 1	3
week 1	4
week 2	almost 5
week 3	5
week 4	almost 6
week 5	6

What to Do

1. Discuss with the children how they have grown and that all living things grow. Select the animal(s) to be observed and discuss with children how to measure the amount of growth with interlocking cubes and with the balance.

2. Have the children make the first measurements, one for length and one for mass. Record this information on the growth chart.

3. Continue taking measurements every few days. Pace the activity according to the growth rate of the animal being observed.

4. When the animals have grown significantly, have the children summarize the growth they've observed with drawings and written or dictated comments.

Assessing the Activity

During the large-group discussion when the animals are being measured, talk about animals and how they grow. Question individual students to determine their understanding whenever they are near the animals being measured.

Science Concept

Animals are living organisms that breathe, move, grow, and require nourishment.

Science Process Skill

To focus observations by using the senses.

Science Vocabulary

balance
chart
growth
longer
mass
maximum
measure
weigh

ACTIVITY 3

What Does Our Animal Smell?

Materials

non-aquatic animals

What Does Our Animal Smell? Discovery Chart

cotton swabs

odorous agents, such as vinegar, lemon, peppermint, pine, orange peel, and vanilla

vials, labeled and capped

For many animals, the sense of smell is the most important sense. We have all seen pets sniff to find food or search diligently in a new pen or cage with their noses. Animals and humans do not smell odors in the same way; the odor of fresh strawberries does not mean the same thing to a hamster as it does to a person. In this activity children will focus their observation skills on the smelling activities of animals and then conduct a simple investigation. They will try to determine the smell reactions of one or more of the animals.

Before the Activity

Prepare the set of odorous agents and the Discovery Chart. Place a number of animals in the Discovery Center. Use any animal that can be placed out for a short time, except for water-dwelling animals. Some animals will require special treatment. For example, earthworms must be kept damp, so the investigation should be conducted on a wet paper towel. Mealworms, sow bugs, and snails also may be used.

C･O･N･N･E･C･T･I･O･N･S

To Language

Expressive Language - Children will explore animal reactions and then share what they discover with others. Encourage the children to share their observations of the response to the odors with you and other children.

To Math

Classifying and Charting - Children will classify a variety of animals into different groups according to their reactions to odors. Their results are recorded in a class chart.

What Does Our Animal Smell?										
animal	lemon		vinegar		orange		peppermint		pine	
	yes	no	yes	no	yes	no	yes	no	yes	no

What to Do

1. Introduce children to the odors they will be using in the experiment. To do this, place a drop of the essence on a cotton swab, and hold it near a volunteer's nose. With your hand, waft the odor toward the child's nose. Ask the other children to make these observations: Does the child react to the smell? Does he or she move close to or away from the smell? Say: The animal may do the same. The animal will be attracted to some odors, not attracted to or repelled from others, and some will make no difference. Ask: Do you think the animals will smell [name of odor]? Challenge the children to explore and find out.

2. Place the odorous agents and cotton swabs in the Discovery Center. Show the group how to wet the swab (use a different swab for each odor) with the agent and to place it near the animal so that the animal can react to the odor. Start about 30 centimeters away and move slowly toward the animal. Stop about 5 centimeters from the animal and wait for a reaction. The animal will move toward an essence that it is attracted to. You might want to discuss with the children the importance of keeping the swabs next to their vials.

3. Encourage the children to closely observe the animals smelling. Have them make a mark on the appropriate place on the chart indicating the reaction for each essence.

4. Send home Animal Family Connection Activity 4 (page 289).

Assessing the Activity

Each child should be able to state two to four odors to which the animals react.

Science Concept

Animals interact with their environment.

Science Process Skill

To focus observations by using the senses.

Science Vocabulary

centimeter
essence
extract
odor
react
repel
respond
smell

CHECKPOINT

Sorting a Sea Full of Shells

Materials (per group)

large-square graph paper
crayons or tape
variety of shells: snail, flat, conch, mollusk, and abalone

Seashells are fun to collect, observe, and sort. They are artistic expression of nature that can be held in the hand. Support children's fascination with them by allowing the children the opportunity to sort and group another collection of shells. The variety of shells the children can experience will be limited only by the number of shells in your collection.

Before the Activity

Obtain some duplicate shells; larger and smaller duplicates would be ideal. The more variety in the shell collection, the more comparisons the children will be able to make.

What to Do

1. Give a shell collection to each group of four children.

2. Encourage the children to observe the attributes of the shells.

3. Request that groups choose one attribute and to group the shells into piles according to that attribute. Some common attributes are length, shape, size, color, and texture.

C▪O▪N▪N▪E▪C▪T▪I▪O▪N▪S

To Language

Expressive Language - Children will verbalize observable attributes as they sort and group shells.

To Math

Counting, Classifying, and Graphing - Children will count the shells contained in the various groups and construct a graph for each classification scheme used to group the shells.

Science Concept

Animals display physical and behavioral diversity.

Science Process Skill

To organize and communicate observations.

Science Vocabulary

attributes
characteristics
classify
graph
group
sort

4. This is another time to expose children to the use of bar graphs as a way of communicating the variety of attributes they found for each of the groupings. Give each group a piece of graph paper. Help them label the horizontal axis with the selected attributes. Have them place each shell in the correct column and either tape each shell into one box or color one box for each shell.

Assessing the Activity

Are the children able to choose several attributes and then sort the shells accurately? Are they able to complete the bar graph and identify the attributes selected?

Plants

Essential Information

Most plants have the same basic structure: roots, stems, leaves, flowers, and seeds. Even young children can learn to identify these parts of a plant.

Roots

Roots have several roles. They anchor the plant to the ground. They absorb water and minerals from the soil. Some roots store food for the plant. Some plants have special roots that allow them to survive in hostile environments (air roots in cypress and mangroves), to support themselves (prop roots in corn), or to absorb water from the air (aerial roots in orchids).

Roots are of two main types: taproots and fibrous roots. Dandelions and carrots have taproots, while grasses have fibrous roots. A single rye grass fibrous system may grow fourteen million roots and rootlets, which, if lined up, can reach 640 km (400 mi.).

Science Concepts

The following science concepts will be addressed in the Plants Unit:

1. Plants have a great diversity of physical characteristics

2. Plants are living organisms that require water, light, and nourishment for growth and survival.

3. Plants change throughout their life cycles, and they grow and reproduce.

Getting Ready

Add the following materials to the Discovery Center:

- a variety of plants, including at least one in bloom
- potting soil, clay soil, and sand
- planting containers, such as paper cups, margarine tubs, fast-food containers, and egg cartons
- artificial plants, both silk and plastic
- assorted seeds, such as lima, radish, mung beans, grass, corn, and peas
- watering bottles, including a spray bottle for watering small plants
- resealable plastic bags
- collection of dried herbs
- baby food jars
- masking tape
- broom and dust pan
- dish pans or similar containers to hold soil
- camera for documenting changes in plants over time (optional)

Note: You will need to plant marigold seeds for Focusing Observations Activity 6, Plants Grow from Seeds, before beginning the Plants unit (preferably, 3 weeks before). Note on a calendar the day you plant the seeds.

Stems

Stems support leaves and lift them to the sunlight. They bear the cones, flowers, and fruit. Stems conduct water, food, and minerals from the roots to the flowers and leaves. They also bring food in the form of sap throughout the plant and down to the roots. Stems can be fleshy as in celery or corn, or woody as in a tree, shrub, or vine. In woody plants, layers form each year that produce tree rings, which can be used to determine a plant's age. Stems vary in size and shape from huge tree trunks to the stems of tiny flowers.

Leaves

Leaves are the food-production sites of the plant. All green parts of the plant contain chlorophyll and are where photosynthesis takes place. On the underside of most leaves are openings where gases (carbon dioxide, oxygen, and water vapor) are exchanged. Leaves vary in size from the 1-millimeter duckweed to the South American water lily, which can grow up to 2 meters across.

Flowers and Seeds

Flowers are the reproductive organs of the plant. The parts of a flower vary in their size and structure and are one of the characteristics used to identify plants. A flower must be pollinated for seeds to form. Pollen is usually carried by the wind or by animals such as bees and hummingbirds. After pollination, a fruit will develop. Inside the fruit are seeds that will form new plants. When a seed is dispersed and lands in a suitable environment, it will germinate (sprout) and grow into a new plant.

To give children a rich experience, expose them to a great diversity of plant life. It is also a valuable experience for them to be aware of the collection process, rather than having everything just appear in the classroom.

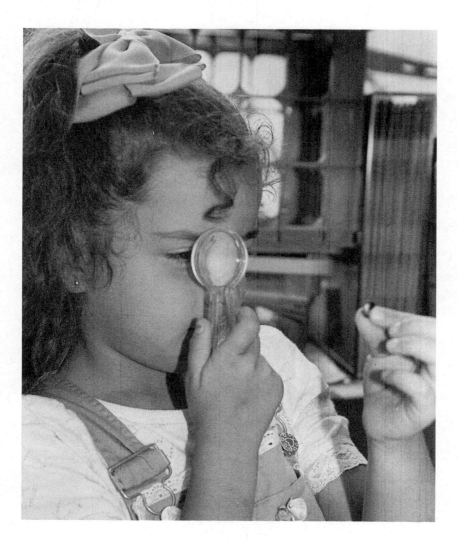

Materials

large sheet of newsprint (for a Discovery Chart)

markers

tape

plant materials

Success in Science Inventory

Discovery Journals

There are more than seven hundred poisonous plants, including as poison ivy, poison oak, poison sumac, holly, lily of the valley, and iris. Be aware of this and carefully screen all plants brought into the classroom. Also be aware of children who are allergic to certain plants. Check school records and with families for this information.

You may want to send a letter to families to announce the Plants unit (see the Family Connection, page 290, for an example). Ask families to contribute plants, planting containers, and other related supplies. Contact community resources, such as florists and nursery workers, that may be willing to contribute materials, expertise, or a field trip site. Consider including herbs, cacti, flowering plants, plants with unusual shapes and textures, and maybe even a Venus flytrap. Keep a record of the materials collected and the sources.

If your classroom has little natural light, you may want to consider using grow lights. Ask the families; someone may have grow lights available for loan. Do not buy what you do not have to buy!

Free Discovery

When beginning this unit, plant various seeds to have living plants available for activities. Plant bean seeds in advance for use in Focusing Observations Activities 13 and 14 (Lighten Up and Find the Light). Plant marigold seeds early for use in Focusing Observations Activity 6 (Plants Grow from Seeds).

You may want to use the SSI and Discovery Journal entries to evaluate the children's progress during Free Discovery.

> What We Know About Plants
> They need sun to grow.
> They need food to grow.
> They have different colors.
> Plants have their own names.
> Different plants look different.
> Some plants smell.
> Some plants give you poisonous ivy.

What to Do

1. With the children, prepare a Discovery chart entitled What Do We Know About Plants?

2. Before the children handle the plants, review the following safety rules with them.

   - Do not rub sap from a plant or juice from a fruit on your skin or allow it to touch open wounds.

   - Do not pick wildflowers or cultivated plants that you can not identify.

   - Always wash your hands thoroughly after handling plants.

3. Begin Free Discovery. Have the children work at the Discovery Center, and encourage them to write and draw about their discoveries in their Discovery Journals.

4. Record individual performance using the Success in Science Inventory.

5. Reassemble the class. Restate the comments recorded on the Discovery Chart, and ask the children to share drawings and writings from their Discovery Journals. Add the new information to the Discovery Chart in a different color. Call the children's attention to the new discoveries they have made during their free exploration. Then ask: What else would you like to learn about plants?

Story Time

Use this story-telling activity to raise the children's interest in plants.

The Surprise Garden

Once, in a town not very far from here, there lived a group of boys and girls just about your size. These children were always up to something, and usually it would get them into trouble. Like the time they decided that the school building wasn't very pretty and so one afternoon they got together and painted flowers all over the outside of the building. Boy, did they get in trouble! Mr. Wilson, their kindergarten teacher, made them wash all the paint off the building. It took them about ten days to finish that job.

Another time they wondered what they would look like if they were bald and so—you guessed it!—they cut off each other's hair.

Uh oh! Their parents were *furious*! Everyone kept asking them why they couldn't do something nice. They really didn't mean to be naughty; they just couldn't help it.

Week after week the children thought up something different to do, and it always got them into trouble. Early in the spring, one of the children, _____, had a new idea. "Hey everybody, what if we do something that won't get us into trouble? I'm really tired of making my mom cry all the time."

The other kids all nodded in agreement; it really wasn't fun to have all the grownups mad all the time.

"What do you have in mind?" asked one boy.

The child said, "Why don't we make a secret garden. Then, when all the vegetables are grown, we'll have a big party for the whole town."

All of the children rushed home that day and gathered up all the gardening tools they could find. Each child got a packet of seeds from a parent and they met at _____'s house early the next morning. They found a garden spot up in the hills that was high and dry and they immediately went to work.

Every day when they weren't in school they were working in the garden. They would sing and laugh as they worked. Their parents were a little confused, but happy because the children weren't getting into trouble anymore. But no one knew what they were doing instead!

Late that spring, rains came. Day and night it rained and rained. Each day though, one of the children would check the garden, and it was still okay. Soon, though, the town became flooded. The people of the town were very sad. It was going to take all of them to clean up the town and all of the homes and businesses.

One night a town meeting was called so they could decide what they were going to do. Everyone was there—except the children, but no one really noticed.

Suddenly, there came a loud banging and clanging. Into the town meeting marched the children in bright costumes pulling wagons *full* of beautiful vegetables and fruits. There were wagons of tomatoes and potatoes, onions and carrots, lettuce and beets, cauliflower and peppers, and even a wagon full of strawberries!

The people of the town jumped up and ran to them. "Children, where did you get this wonderful food?"

_____ stepped forward and proudly explained, "We grew it all by ourselves, and it is our gift to all of you because we love you."

The townspeople were so happy and proud of the children. Mr. Wilson spoke for the whole town when he said, "Thank you children! You are the nicest, best children in the whole, wide world!"

ACTIVITY 1

Draw a Plant

Materials

crayons or markers
Discovery Journals

Introduce this activity immediately following Free Discovery. This activity will help children focus their attention on the physical characteristics of plants they have observed. It will also document each child's starting point in his or her understanding of plants, giving both you and the children a reference point for seeing growth throughout the unit.

Before the Activity

Remove or cover all plants used during Free Discovery.

C▪O▪N▪N▪E▪C▪T▪I▪O▪N▪S

To Language

Expressive Language - Children will listen to one another as they share their drawings.

Discovery Journals - Children will tell you about their drawings as you write dictated descriptions.

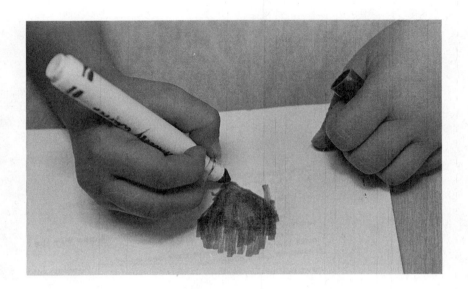

Science Concept

Plants have a great diversity of physical characteristics.

Science Process Skill

To focus observations by using the senses.

Science Vocabulary

descriptive words about plants, such as big, little, small, shiny, prickly, fuzzy, tall, and long plant

What to Do

1. Ask the children to draw pictures of a plant from memory in their Discovery Journals. The drawings may be of any of the plants they have observed and used during Free Discovery or a plant they remember from their home or outdoors.

2. As the children complete their drawings, they can dictate a description of the plant for you to write captions. They may also make their own captions at their own level of literacy.

3. Use these drawings for future reference and for comparison when the children complete the Checkpoint activity, Draw a Plant Again (page 222).

Assessing the Activity

Look at the drawings and the captions. Do they reflect some knowledge of plants?

ACTIVITY 2

Leaf Rubbings

Materials

paper
crayons without paper wrappings
variety of leaves
large sheet of newsprint
tape

Leaves come in many shapes and sizes. Each plant species has a unique leaf structure, an identifying characteristic. Making leaf rubbings allows the children to observe and compare leaves in a new way. They will discover that the structure of leaves can be similar to a circle, triangle, square, or rectangle. The final artwork is fun to share.

Before the Activity

Take the children on a leaf-collecting walk. Gather leaves of different sizes and shapes.

What to Do

1. Demonstrate how to make a leaf rubbing by placing a leaf, underside up, under a piece of paper and rubbing over the paper with the side of a crayon.

2. Have the children select paper, crayons, and leaves to make their own rubbings. Because many of the leaves will be small, the children can make more than one rubbing on each sheet of paper. Give them plenty of time to experiment with making leaf rubbings.

C ∙ O ∙ N ∙ N ∙ E ∙ C ∙ T ∙ I ∙ O ∙ N ∙ S

To Language

Expressive Language - Children will describe and compare the shape, size, and structure attributes of leaf rubbings.

To Math

Comparing and Graphing - Children will compare leaves by size, shape, or some other physical property, and generate a class chart of the leaf observations.

Science Concept

Plants have a great diversity of physical characteristics.

Science Process Skill

To focus observations by using the senses.

Science Vocabulary

descriptive words about the shapes and sizes of leaves, such as alike, different, oval, size, shape, diamond, rectangle, round, square, and triangle

3. When the children are finished, ask them to share their art. Focus the discussion on the sizes, shapes, and features of the leaves.

   Display the rubbings on a wall.

4. Observe and compare the variety of shapes that are revealed. Talk about how many leaves have rectangular, round, triangular, or other shapes. Help the children make a class chart that indicates the number of leaves in each shape category.

5. Send home Plants Family Connection Activity 1 (page 291).

Assessing the Activity

As the children describe and compare their rubbings, they should make reference to specific attributes, such as shape, size, and structure.

ACTIVITY 3

Color Me Green

Materials

leaves
paper
Discovery Journals

Although almost all plants contain green chlorophyll, there is a great deal of diversity in their coloration. Plants stains allow us to compare plants in another way: some leaves may leave a yellow, brown, or orange stain, and leaves and stems of the same plant may leave different color stains.

Before the Activity

Take the children on a leaf-gathering walk to gather an assortment of leaves. (You may also want to use leaves from plants growing in the classroom.) Look for leaves that might produce unexpected results. For example, the house plant Swedish ivy produces an orange stain.

What to Do

1. Ask the children to talk about times when they have stained their clothes or bodies. Ask: Where did the stains came from? Were they food spills? Grass stains? Were all the stains the same color?

2. Demonstrate how to make a leaf stain. Crush a leaf and rub it firmly onto a sheet of paper until it makes a large, dark stain. Explain to the children that making a stain in this way is one way to observe a plant.

C·O·N·N·E·C·T·I·O·N·S

To Language

Expressive Language - Children will be using words such as *dark* and *light* to describe the shading of each leaf stain.

To Math

Comparing - Children will compare the various colors of leaf stains.

Science Concept

Plants have a great diversity of physical characteristics.

Science Process Skill

To focus observations by using the senses.

Science Vocabulary

chlorophyll
dark
leaf
light
pigment
plant names
stain

3. Tell the children to make leaf stains on a page of their Discovery Journals. Warn them to be careful of staining their clothing.

4. Dried stains may look different from fresh stains. As a stain dries, have the children watch for changes.

5. Direct the children to look at the shades of green in the stains. Ask: Are the stains alike or different? Light or dark in shading? Are there any stains that are not green?

Assessing the Activity

Examine the stains in the children's Discovery Journals. Can the children indicate which ones are dark and which are light? Do they understand that different plants make different stains?

ACTIVITY 4

How Tall Are Plants?

Materials

crayons
interlocking cubes
plants
chart with a column for each plant to be observed
Discovery Journals

Height is another physical characteristic of plants. In this activity children compare the heights of plants by using interlocking cubes, a unit of measure easy for them to use.

Before the Activity

Select four plants of varying heights. Mark the plants with the letters A, B, C, and D. You may also want to label them with the plant names.

What to Do

1. Have the children observe the four plants. Talk with them about the most accurate way to measure plants. Ask: Where do you start? How would you measure vines? How would you measure plants with more than one stem? Develop group guidelines for measuring, such as beginning to measure from where the plant emerges from the soil and measuring the longest or tallest part of the plant.

2. Demonstrate how to measure plants using interlocking cubes. On a sheet of paper taped to the wall, demonstrate how to trace around the cubes to make a bar graph. Label the four columns A, B, C, and D, corresponding to each plant.

C ▪ O ▪ N ▪ N ▪ E ▪ C ▪ T ▪ I ▪ O ▪ N ▪ S

To Language

Expressive Language - Children will share observations of plant size, measure and compare different types of plants, and record their findings.

To Math

Counting, Measuring, and Comparing - Children will count interlocking cubes as they make their measurements to compare and chart the results.

3. With the children, count the number of cubes in each of the bars and write that number above the bar.

4. Place other plants in the Discovery Center and have the children work in groups of four to measure the heights of the plants and to trace the cubes to make bar graphs in their Discovery Journals. Explain that there will be some differences in the measurements depending on how each group measures the plants.

Science Concept

Plants have a great diversity of physical characteristics.

Science Process Skill

To focus observations by using the senses.

Science Vocabulary

comparative terms, such as tall, short, big, small
different
grow
height
plant
same

How Tall Are We?

12

10

6

5

Plant Key
A. Geranium
B. Azalea
C. Cactus
D. Philodendron

A   B   C   D

Assessing the Activity

Check the drawings in the Discovery Journals. Make a general comparison of the children's measurements to your own findings. Be willing to accept variation in measurements.

The variety and multitude of colors in plants are part of the reason people enjoy them. This activity will help the children develop awareness of the many colors of plants and will put their observing and recording skills to use.

ACTIVITY 5

What Colors Are Plants?

Materials

crayons
variety of plants
Discovery Journals

The variety and multitude of colors in plants are part of the reason people enjoy them. This activity will help the children develop awareness of the many colors of plants and will put their observing and recording skills to use.

Before the Activity

For this activity include some plants with colorful blooms or leaves, such as coleus, begonias, and impatiens. The greater the variety of colors, the more interesting the activity.

What to Do

1. Ask: How many different colors can we find in our room? What colors are on our clothes?

2. Ask: How many colors can we find on plants? Discuss the various colors of plants with the children. Ask: Are all green plants the same shade of green?

3. Direct the children's attention to the plants in the Discovery Center. Ask: How many colors can we find in each plant?

C▪O▪N▪N▪E▪C▪T▪I▪O▪N▪S

To Language

Expressive Language - Children will talk about the colors they see in the classroom, their clothing, and plants.

To Math

Grouping - Children will separate plants into groups according to color and draw pictures indicating plant color.

Science Concept

Plants have a great diversity of
physical characteristics.

Science Process Skill

To focus observations by using the
senses.

Science Vocabulary

chlorophyll
pigment
plant names

4. As children identify colors, ask them to use crayons to make
   drawings with those colors in their Discovery Journals. For
   example, for begonia they might make drawings with pink,
   yellow, and two shades of green.

Assessing the Activity

Pick a plant with a variety of colors. Have the children observe
and record the colors in the plant. Do they indicate an awareness
of the variety of colors in plants?

CHECKPOINT

Draw a Plant Again

Materials

crayons
Discovery Journals

This activity will ask the children to again draw a plant from memory as a way of documenting their growing understanding of plant structure.

Before the Activity

Cover or remove the classroom plants.

C·O·N·N·E·C·T·I·O·N·S

To Language

Expressive Language - Children will freely express themselves as they share the plant drawings from their Discovery Journals.

Discovery Journals - Children will caption their drawings at their own level.

To Math

Comparing - Children will compare the physical characteristics of their plant drawing to the drawings of other children.

Science Concept

Plants have a great diversity of physical characteristics.

Science Process Skill

To focus observations by using the senses.

Science Vocabulary

names of plant parts
plant names

What to Do

1. Ask the children to draw in their Discovery Journals, from memory, a picture of a plant.

2. Have the children write something about their drawing. They may write at their own level or dictate to you.

3. Have them compare their second drawings to their first from Focusing Observations Activity 1, Draw a Plant. Discuss the changes that have occurred in the two pictures of the plants. Ask open-ended questions that support the expression of the children's own thoughts and feelings, such as: Why do you like the begonia flowers?

Assessing the Activity

The drawings and the oral exchange will indicate the children's awareness of the physical characteristics of plants. Do the children's representations include more detail than their previous drawings?

ACTIVITY 6

Plants Grow from Seeds

Materials

marigold seeds, which were planted prior to the beginning of the Plants unit

calendar

planting containers

water bottles

potting soil

Discovery Journals

large sheet of newsprint (optional)

camera

film

This activity will enable the children to observe the life cycle of a plant. They will plant seeds, care for the plants, watch them grow to maturity, and see them produce seeds for the next generation. This entire process will take 40 to 48 days, depending on soil, temperature, and light conditions, and will be an ongoing part of the Plants unit. Take photographs throughout this activity to prepare for the Checkpoint activity for this section, Changes (page 232).

Before the Activity

Plant the seeds 3 weeks before the Plants unit begins (see page 206). Note on the calendar the day the seeds are planted. Clear a place for the plants to be kept for about 6 weeks. Seeds will germinate in less than 12 hours, plants will emerge from the soil in 48 hours, flower buds will appear in 7 to 8 days, flowers will begin to open in 12 to 13 days, and seeds may be harvested in 40 to 48 days. Remind the children to water the plants as needed.

C▪O▪N▪N▪E▪C▪T▪I▪O▪N▪S

To Language

Calendar - Children will record their observations of the plant's growth cycle according to the passage of time on a calendar.

Expressive Language - Observing plants as they grow from seed is an exciting process that should stimulate much language development as the children discuss and record what they see happening.

Discovery Journals - Children will document the plant life cycle.

Science Concept

Plants change throughout their life cycle, and they grow and reproduce.

Science Process Skill

To focus observations by using the senses.

Science Vocabulary

growth
life cycle
plant
seeds
sprout

What to Do

1. Focus the children's attention on the plants throughout the unit. Direct them to watch for growth daily. As observable changes occur, have the children count the number of days that have passed and draw the plants in their Discovery Journals, dictating descriptive words for their drawings. Encourage the children to add captions at their level of literacy.

2. After observing the entire life cycle of the plants (40 to 48 days), suggest that the children collect the seeds from these plants. To do this, have them pull the petals from a dried blossom to reveal a cluster of seeds. You may want to make a Discovery Chart showing the various stages of growth.

3. Ask the children to take collected seeds, to plant and care for them, and to observe new plants. The children will see that plants reproduce their own seeds and the life cycle continues.

Assessing the Activity

Children should be able to infer that seeds produce plants and that plants are grown from seeds.

ACTIVITY 7

Seeds or Nonseeds: Which Grow Better?

Materials

radish, corn, lima bean, and grass seeds

nonseed plant material, such as leaves and other plant parts that will not grow

wood, plastic, rocks, and other things the children want to plant

prepared planting containers

tape or glue

sheet of newsprint

Through the process of observation, the children will understand that not all things that are planted, watered, and given light will grow.

What to Do

1. Have the children examine a variety of seeds and nonseed material. Make a Discovery Chart of what the children think will and will not grow. Glue or tape a sample of the item to the chart.

2. Invite groups of two or four children to plant seeds and nonseed materials in separate planting containers, to label the

C▪O▪N▪N▪E▪C▪T▪I▪O▪N▪S

To Language

Expressive Language - Children will explain why they think particular items will or will not grow.

To Math

Grouping - Children will sort and group a selection of seed and nonseed materials.

Science Concept

Plants change throughout their life cycle, and they grow and reproduce.

Science Process Skill

To focus observations by using the senses.

Science Vocabulary

grow
kinds
living
nonliving
seeds
variety

containers with names, drawings, or samples of the objects, and to place them in a warm location and water them as needed.

3. After several days they should begin to see results in some of the containers. Talk about the results with the children. How accurate were their predictions?

4. Ask: Can you create a rule about growing plants?

5. As an extension, you may want to give the children the opportunity to propagate plants through stem cuttings.

6. Send home Plants Family Connection Activity 2 (page 291).

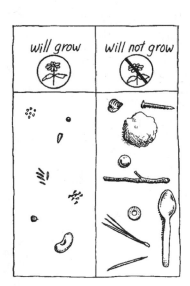

Assessing the Activity

Children should be able to infer that plants can grow from a variety of seeds but that they will not grow from nonseed material.

ACTIVITY 8

Seed Exploration

Materials

magnifying glasses
lima beans
Discovery Journals

Seeds have several parts. In this activity the children will look inside a seed. They will discover that a seed has a baby plant (embryo), food for the embryo's growth, and that the embryo and its food are protected by an outer covering.

Before the Activity

Soak the beans in water for 24 hours prior to the activity.

What to Do

1. Ask the children what they think the inside of a seed looks like.

2. Give each child a bean.

3. Demonstrate this dissection procedure:

    a. Peel off the outer skin (seed coat) of the lima bean.

    b. Split the lima bean in half lengthwise.

    c. Identify the following seed parts:

    Seed coat (outer protection of seed)

    Embryo (root system and shoot system will grow from the embryo)

    Food storage area

C ▪ O ▪ N ▪ N ▪ E ▪ C ▪ T ▪ I ▪ O ▪ N ▪ S

To Language

Expressive Language - Children will talk about what they see as they dissect and examine seed parts.

Discovery Journals - Children will label their drawings at their own level of literacy.

Science Concept

Plants change throughout their life cycle, and they grow and reproduce.

Science Process Skill

To focus observations by using the senses.

Science Vocabulary

baby plant
embryo (baby plant)
food
protection
seed
seed coat
seedling
seed parts

4. Invite the children to dissect their own seeds and to use magnifying glasses to get a closer look.

5. Have the children make drawings in their Discovery Journals of the dissected seed. Assist the children in labeling the seed parts.

Assessing the Activity

The children's drawings should make reference to each of the seed's parts.

ACTIVITY 9

Plant Anatomy

Materials

crayons
live plant, in bloom
trowel
containers
Discovery Journals

All plants have structural parts in common. Human beings have body parts, such as a head, trunk, and limbs. Plants have roots, stems, leaves, and perhaps flowers. In this activity the children will examine a plant's many parts and the functions of each.

What to Do

1. Ask the children: What body parts do you have? (head, arm, legs, feet, and so on). Say: We are going to look at the many parts that make up a plant. Plants have parts just as your body has parts.

2. Place the plant on a table in front of the children. Identify and discuss the basic parts of the plant, and discuss the function of each.

   a. *Roots* anchor and support the plant, take in water and food, and store food. (Gently lift the plant root ball from the pot so that children can observe the roots.)

   b. *Stems* holds leaves up to the light and move water and food up and down the plant.

   c. *Leaves* "catch" light and use it to make food.

   d. *Flowers* produce seeds and attract birds, insects, and other pollinators.

C ▪ O ▪ N ▪ N ▪ E ▪ C ▪ T ▪ I ▪ O ▪ N ▪ S

To Language

Expressive Language - Children will use science vocabulary as they compare their own bodies to various plant parts.

Discovery Journals - Children will label their drawings at their own level of literacy.

Science Concept

Plants change throughout their life cycle, and they grow and reproduce.

Science Process Skill

To focus observations by using the senses.

Science Vocabulary

body
flower
fruit
leaf
plant
root
seed
stem

3. Ask: In what ways are our bodies like plants?

4. Take the children on a walk to a lot or roadside where weeds are plentiful. Dig up a few plants that demonstrate various plant parts. Emphasize that you are taking just a few plants because it is important to conserve them.

5. Return to the classroom, and have the children draw in their Discovery Journals the collected weed samples. Assist them in labeling the plant parts.

6. As an extension, you could take the children on a neighborhood walk. Challenge them to identify parts of the plants they find. For example, they may not realize that trees are plants that grow from seeds and have roots, stems, and leaves.

Assessing the Activity

The children's drawings should include the plant parts you have discussed.

CHECKPOINT

Changes

Materials

4 to 6 plants
camera (preferably an instant camera)
film
4 to 6 sheets of newsprint

Time passing is a concept that young children can grasp, especially when it is observed in an easily understood format. In this activity the children will take photographs of plants during the various stages of growth. The photographs will document clearly the changes that occur during the growth cycle.

Before the Activity

Choose plants that are distinctive. Also, use the photographs you took in Activity 6, Plants Grow from Seeds (page 224).

C▪O▪N▪N▪E▪C▪T▪I▪O▪N▪S

To Language

Expressive Language - Children will talk about changes that have been recorded on film over the 40- to 48-day time frame.

Written Language - Children will dictate comments on observable changes and record them on a Discovery Chart.

Science Concept

Plants change throughout their life cycle, and they grow and reproduce.

Science Process Skill

To focus observations by using the senses.

Science Vocabulary

flower
grow
life cycle
light
plant
roots
seeds
stem
sun
water

What to Do

1. You and the children take turns photographing the plants at least once a week for a month. The photographs will illustrate time passing and the changes that result from growth.

2. Prepare a Discovery Chart for each plant, using the photographs and the children's comments about the changes they have observed. Ask questions, such as: When did the plant break through the soil? When did it first show buds? Leaves?

Assessing the Activity

After experiencing this activity, children will have a pictorial and written reference that will show how plants grow and change. As children look at the pictures, they should be able to point out changes taking place in the plants over time.

ACTIVITY 10

Which One Is Alive?

Materials

1 live plant
1 plastic or silk plant
large sheet of newsprint

Children need to understand the difference between real and artificial plants before they can effectively explore factors that are necessary for life. Artificial plants are often so realistic that even adults have a hard time telling whether the plants are alive. This activity is an opportunity for children to explore the differences between living and nonliving plants.

Before the Activity

Choose a live plant that is hardy enough to withstand constant handling. Prepare a large Living/Nonliving Discovery Chart.

What to Do

1. Place both plants in the Discovery Center. Encourage children to use the senses of touch, sight, and smell to observe differences in the plants.

2. Discuss with the children the differences they found in living and nonliving plants.

3. Record their observations on the Discovery Chart. When the chart is complete, read it back to the children.

C·O·N·N·E·C·T·I·O·N·S

To Language

Expressive Language - Support the children as they verbalize their thoughts about the differences between artificial and live plants. You will hear them use the word *fake* often. Ask them to stretch their imaginations as they find words to describe textures and smells.

Plant	How It Looks	How It Smells	How It Feels
Living			
Nonliving			

Assessing the Activity

Listen to the differences that the children dictate for the Discovery Chart. Are they accurate?

Science Concept

Plants are living organisms that require water, light, and nourishment for growth and survival.

Science Process Skill

To focus observations by using the senses.

Science Vocabulary

artificial
living
nonliving

ACTIVITY 11

Plants Need Water

Materials (per child or group)

quick-sprouting seeds, such as radish, grass, or mung bean

2 planting containers

dry potting soil

masking tape

marker

water bottles

Discovery Journals

Seeds need water (and warmth) to sprout. By comparing the results of seeds planted with and without moisture, the children will discover this fact.

Before the Activity

Fill planting containers with potting soil, two for each child or group. The soil must be dry: moisture in damp soil may cause unwatered seeds to sprout. With masking tape, label one container Water and one No Water (or Yes and No). An illustration, such as empty and full glasses of water, or a drop of water and a drop of water with an X through it, could also be used.

What to Do

1. Have the children plant seeds in the containers and then put the containers aside in a warm place. Avoid locations, such as near windows, that get cold at night.

2. Direct the children to water the containers marked Water but not to water the containers marked No Water.

C▪O▪N▪N▪E▪C▪T▪I▪O▪N▪S

To Language

Expressive Language - Discussion will focus on the effect of water on plant growth.

Discovery Journals - Children will write or dictate captions for their drawings.

To Math

Counting and Recording Time - Children will record observations in chronological order, and might count days since the seeds were planted.

Science Concept

Plants are living organisms that require water, light, and nourishment for growth and survival.

Science Process Skill

To focus observations by using the senses.

Science Vocabulary

grow
light
moisture
plant
sprout
sprout
survival
water

3. Have the children observe both containers daily until the seeds sprout. Every two or three days ask them to draw in their Discovery Journals what they observe. Have them write or dictate captions for their drawings. You might have them keep track of the number of days since they planted the seeds.

4. Discuss this activity with the children. Ask: Can you think of a rule (hypothesis) about seeds' need for water?

5. You may want to save these plants for use in other activities.

Assessing the Activity

Both the children's discussion and Discovery Journal entries should be consistent with your observations. Children should be able to make the inference that water is needed for seed sprouting.

ACTIVITY 12

Just Enough or Too Much?

Materials

3 potted blooming plants, such as begonias, impatiens, or petunias

water bottle

bowl, large enough to submerge the pot of one plant

Discovery Journals

Plants, like other organisms, need water to live. The classroom plants must be watered. Overwatering, however, fills the air spaces in the soil and can rot or kill the plants. This activity will allow children to investigate the effects that varied amounts of water have on plants. You may wish to do this activity concurrently with the next activity, Lighten Up.

What to Do

1. Talk about the human body's need for water to grow and stay healthy. Ask: How do we let other people know we are thirsty?

2. Discuss how plants need water, as do humans, to grow and stay healthy. Ask: How do we know when a plant needs water? Explain that it is important not to give most plants *too* much water, as that can be as harmful as too little water.

C▪O▪N▪N▪E▪C▪T▪I▪O▪N▪S

To Language

Expressive Language - Children will use their science vocabulary as they describe what happens to the plants over the 2-week period.

Discovery Journals - Children will draw and write or dictate captions about their observations of the plants over time.

To Math

Counting and Recording Time - Children will sequence their entries in their Discovery Journals. Children might count and record the number of days that have passed since the investigation began.

Science Concept

Plants are living organisms that require water, light, and nourishment for growth and survival.

Science Process Skill

To focus observations by using the senses.

Science Vocabulary

compare
investigate
rot
water
wilt

3. Set up a simple investigation using the three potted plants, and explain the investigation to the children.

   a. One plant gets no water.

   b. One plant gets water as needed (to be determined by observation of plant and dryness of soil).

   c. One plant is placed into a bowl of water with the soil completely submerged.

4. Over a period of 2 weeks, have the children watch for signs that a plant is getting too much water (yellows, drops leaves and flowers, has stunted growth) and signs that a plant is not getting enough water (wilts, drops leaves, has dry, brittle leaves).

5. Throughout the investigation ask the children to draw observations in their Discovery Journals. You might have them count the number of days that have passed since the investigation began. Have them dictate captions about their observations.

Assessing the Activity

Discuss with the children their observations of the three plants over the 2-week period. Ask questions that focus the children's observations on the effects of varying amounts of water given to plants. Do their responses indicate an understanding of the effects of water on plants?

ACTIVITY 13

Lighten Up

Materials

2 fast-growing green plants, such as beans or tomatoes
large cardboard box
Discovery Journals

Plants make their own food through the process of photosynthesis. To do this, plants need minerals, water, and light. Remove one of these essential elements, and plants will not survive. This activity will enable the children to discover what happens to a plant when light is removed. You may wish to do this activity concurrently with the previous activity, Just Enough or Too Much?

What to Do

1. Ask: What do you think will happen if we do not give a plant light?

2. Place one plant under the covered box and the other close by. Water them adequately, but do not overwater. The plant in the box will probably not need as much water as the other plant. Provide light to the plant in the box only when changes such as yellowing are apparent. Putting the plant in sunlight before such changes are too drastic will allow it to recuperate.

C▪O▪N▪N▪E▪C▪T▪I▪O▪N▪S

To Language

Expressive Language - Children will use their science vocabulary as they observe and talk about the comparisons they make.

Written Language - Children will caption their drawings at their own developmental levels.

Science Concept

Plants are living organisms that require water, light, and nourishment for growth and survival.

Science Process Skill

To focus observations by using the senses.

Science Vocabulary

death
growth
healthy
life

3. After a few days or when there is a noticeable difference, ask the children to compare the plant in the covered box with other plants in the classroom. Ask the children to draw the results of this investigation in their Discovery Journal. Have the children caption their drawings at their own developmental levels.

4. Talk with the children about their observations. Can they make up a rule (hypothesis) about plants and light?

Assessing the Activity

Both the children's discussion and their drawings and captions should indicate their understanding of the effects of light on plant growth. The children should be able to infer that light is needed for plant growth.

ACTIVITY 14

Find the Light

Materials

large cardboard box with lid

scissors

2 fast-growing green plants, such as beans or tomatoes

water

Discovery Journals

Plants need light to grow and to produce food. Most plants react to the stimulus of light and will grow toward it even when the light is dim. In this activity the children will observe that green plants grow toward light. You may wish to do this activity concurrently with the next activity, What Plants Need to Grow.

Before the Activity

Cut a hole for light in one side of the box.

What to Do

1. Encourage the children to talk about different kinds of light, such as sunlight, moonlight, lamp light, and candlelight.

2. As the children watch, water and place one of the plants into the box at the point farthest from the hole. Close the box. Place the other plant in the sunlight, next to the box. Position the box so that the hole faces the sunlight.

3. Every day or so, open the box to water the plant if necessary, and ask the children to observe the direction of plant growth. Ask: What direction are the plant and leaves pointing? You may want to place the plants side by side to make the differences more apparent.

C▪O▪N▪N▪E▪C▪T▪I▪O▪N▪S

To Language

Expressive Language - The children will use the science vocabulary to describe what happens as they observe the plant growing toward light.

Written Language - Children will write or dictate their description of their drawings.

Science Concept

Plants are living organisms that require water, light, and nourishment for growth and survival.

Science Process Skill

To focus observations by using the senses.

Science Vocabulary

compare
response
sunlight

4. Ask the children to compare the growth of the two plants over 2 to 3 weeks. Periodically have them draw the plants in their Discovery Journals. They may write or dictate descriptions of their drawings.

5. Talk with the children about their observations. Can they think of a rule (hypothesis) about plants and light?

Assessing the Activity

Both the children's discussion and Discovery Journals entries should indicate their understanding of the effects of light on plants. They should be able to infer that plants grow toward light.

CHECKPOINT

What Plants Need to Grow

Materials

fast-growing seeds, such as radishes, grass, or alfalfa

potting soil

1 planting container (per group)

water bottle (per group)

large sheet of newsprint

Discovery Journals

The children have been exposed to a variety of activities to help them understand that plants need specific things to grow and survive. This activity will let them use that information and will enable you to determine whether the children have the information they need to care for their own special plants. You may wish to do this activity concurrently with the previous activity, Find the Light.

Before the Activity

Prepare a work area for the children to fill their containers and plant their seeds.

What to Do

1. Have groups of two or four children plant seeds of their choice in a container using their own method.

2. Discuss with the children what they will do to nurture their plants. Make a Discovery Chart listing the factors the children suggest for plant growth, such as light and water. You may also want to use pictures. Ask the children to predict what factors will result in the healthiest plants. Read the chart back to the children. Do they want to add anything?

C ▪ O ▪ N ▪ N ▪ E ▪ C ▪ T ▪ I ▪ O ▪ N ▪ S

To Language

Expressive Language - Growing plants from seeds to full maturity will stimulate a seemingly unending amount of language. Planting and nurturing plants reveal that many factors influence growth and survival. Listen and talk with the children about what they see happening.

Written Language - Children will caption their drawings at their own level of literacy.

3. Tell the children they will care for their own plants and provide the plants what they need to be healthy. Have the children make drawings in their Discovery Journals throughout the growth period to record observable changes. Have them caption their drawings at their own level of literacy.

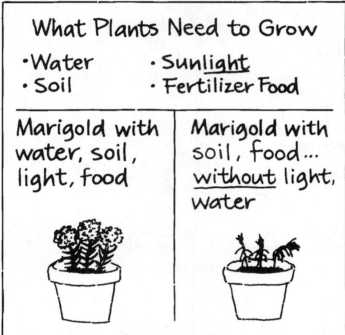

What Plants Need to Grow
- Water
- Soil
- Sunlight
- Fertilizer Food

Marigold with water, soil, light, food	Marigold with soil, food... without light, water

Science Concept

Plants are living organisms that require water, light, and nourishment for growth and survival.

Science Process Skill

To focus observations by using the senses.

Science Vocabulary

compare
growth
height
light
predict
plants
soil
water

4. After about 2 weeks of plant growth, encourage each group to share their project with the rest of the class.

Assessing the Activity

By observing the children's projects and discussing what they are doing to maintain proper growing conditions, you will be able to determine which children understand what a plant needs for growth.

ADDITIONAL STIMULATION

A Plant for Our Class

Materials

This activity provides an opportunity for children to recall and to use the plant-care skills they have learned during the Focusing Observations activities.

Before the Activity

Choose a nursery, florist, or greenhouse to visit, and arrange for someone to talk with the children. Explain to the children that they will be visiting a nursery and will choose a plant for the classroom. Have them discuss questions about plants they might ask. Talk about the classroom's heat, light, and water source, and about what kind of plants would be right for the classroom environment.

What to Do

1. Take a trip to the nursery, florist, or greenhouse. Have the personnel give the children a tour of the facility and describe the various plants.

2. Encourage the children to ask the questions they discussed about choosing a good plant for the classroom and any other questions they may think of. Narrow the choice down to four plants.

C▪O▪N▪N▪E▪C▪T▪I▪O▪N▪S

To Language

Expressive Language - Children will discuss questions they plan to ask the florist, nursery, or greenhouse personnel before choosing a plant for the classroom.

Science Concept

Plants are living organisms that require water, light, and nourishment for growth and survival.

Science Process Skill

To focus observations by using the senses.

Science Vocabulary

light
plant care
plant names
soil
temperature
water

3. Let the children vote for the plant they would like to buy. Purchase the plant and take it back to the classroom, and follow the care instructions provided by the nursery.

4. Rotate the plant-care responsibilities among the children.

Assessing the Activity

Observe that the children give appropriate care to the class plant throughout the school year.

ACTIVITY 1

Living or Nonliving?

Materials

several real plants from the plant collection (per group)

several silk or plastic plants (per group)

dissection tools (plastic knife and scissors)

sheet of newsprint

Through observation the children will recognize similarities and differences among real and artificial plants. They will be able to identify both unique characteristics and characteristics common to both living and nonliving plants.

What to Do

1. Give groups of two or four children several living and non-living plants. Do not identify the plants as living or nonliving.

2. Tell the children to examine the two types of plants. Ask: What differences do you see? How do they smell? How do they feel? In what ways are they the same?

3. Direct them to separate plants they think are living from those they think are nonliving.

C ▪ O ▪ N ▪ N ▪ E ▪ C ▪ T ▪ I ▪ O ▪ N ▪ S

To Language

Expressive Language - As the children examine the living and nonliving plants, they will express how they are using their senses to determine similarities and differences. The Venn diagram will add something new to a print-rich environment.

To Math

Sorting and Classifying - Children will sort plants into two groups and classify them as living or nonliving. They will observe the Venn diagram of characteristics shared by the two groups.

4. Ask: How are real plants and artificial plants alike? How are they different? Record their responses on a Discovery Chart using a Venn diagram.

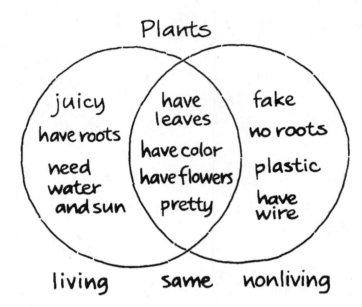

Plants

juicy
have roots
need water and sun

have leaves
have color
have flowers
pretty

fake
no roots
plastic
have wire

living   same   nonliving

Science Concept

Plants are living organisms that require water, light, and nourishment for growth and survival.

Science Process Skill

To use observations to classify objects into groups.

Science Vocabulary

artificial
flower
leaves
living
nonliving
root
stem

Assessing the Activity

Examine the differences that the children have listed for the Discovery Chart. Are they accurate in relation to the items observed? How do they differentiate between living and artificial plants?

ACTIVITY 2

How Do Different Leaves Smell?

Materials

resealable plastic bags

herb samples that have distinctive odors, such as mint, parsley, garlic, chives, oregano, and anise

masking tape

sheet of newsprint

Discovery Journals

Many herbs have unique odors that even young children can learn to distinguish. In this activity children will use their sense of smell to make choices regarding their likes and dislikes of herb odors. This is the beginning of the exploration of smell, taste, and usefulness of herbs in the kitchen.

Before the Activity

Put a small amount of each herb into separate bags. Label the contents of the bags using masking tape. You will need one sample of each herb for each group. Prepare a Discovery Chart with a grid.

What to Do

1. Distribute samples of one herb to each child or group.

2. Tell the children to smell the herb sample, and ask them to describe the odor. Encourage them to verbalize freely and to go beyond *good*, *bad*, and *yuck*. Smells can often elicit memories. Ask: What do you think it smells like? Have you smelled it before? Where?

C▪O▪N▪N▪E▪C▪T▪I▪O▪N▪S

To Language

Expressive Language - Children do not hesitate to let us know how they feel something smells. Children will use vocabulary beyond *good*, *bad*, and *yuck* to describe smells and how they feel about them

Discovery Journals - Children will record their favorite herbs.

To Math

Graphing - Children will help create a bar graph to communicate the results of their vote.

Science Concept

Plants have a great diversity of physical characteristics.

Science Process Skill

To use observations to classify objects into groups.

Science Vocabulary

herb
odor
scent

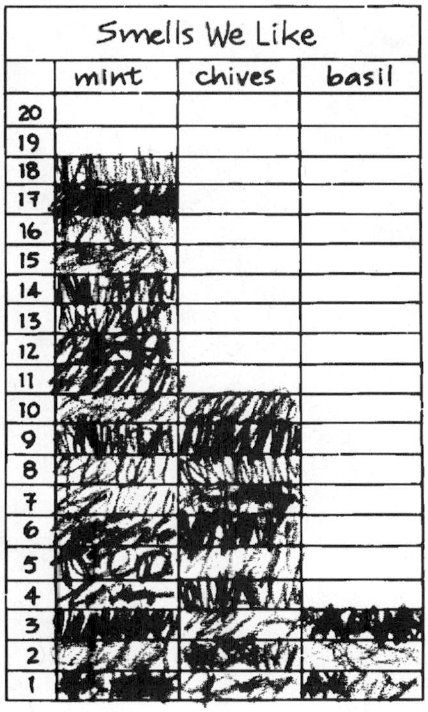

3. Ask: How many like the smell? Record the total on the Discovery Chart. Remind the children that not everyone will feel the same way about each smell. It's good for them to have their own opinions.
4. Repeat the process with each herb.
5. As a final step, have the children draw in their Discovery Journals their favorite herbs.

Assessing the Activity

Children should be able to discuss the voting result of the class and their own opinions.

ACTIVITY 3

Seeds, Seeds, Seeds

Materials (per group)

variety of seeds of different colors, shapes, and sizes

egg cartons

This activity challenges children to demonstrate their recognition of the many attributes of seeds. They will classify seeds according to individual and group properties.

What to Do

1. Give each group of children an egg carton and a variety of seeds.

2. Instruct them to observe the seeds closely. Ask: What colors are the seeds? What shapes? What sizes?

3. Now focus the children's attention on a single seed property, such as size (big versus small). Ask them to put all the small seeds on the right side of their egg carton and all the large seeds on the left side.

4. Continue having them compare properties such as light-colored versus dark-colored seeds, long versus short, thick versus thin, pleasant-smelling versus unpleasant, heavy versus light, and rough versus smooth.

Assessing the Activity

Observe the children as they sort the seeds by different properties. Are they able to classify the objects correctly?

C▪O▪N▪N▪E▪C▪T▪I▪O▪N▪S

To Language

Expressive Language - Children will discuss colors, shapes, sizes, and seed names. (Focus on comparative terms and opposites as the activity progresses.)

To Math

Classification - Children will apply their skills at grouping seeds according to similar characteristics.

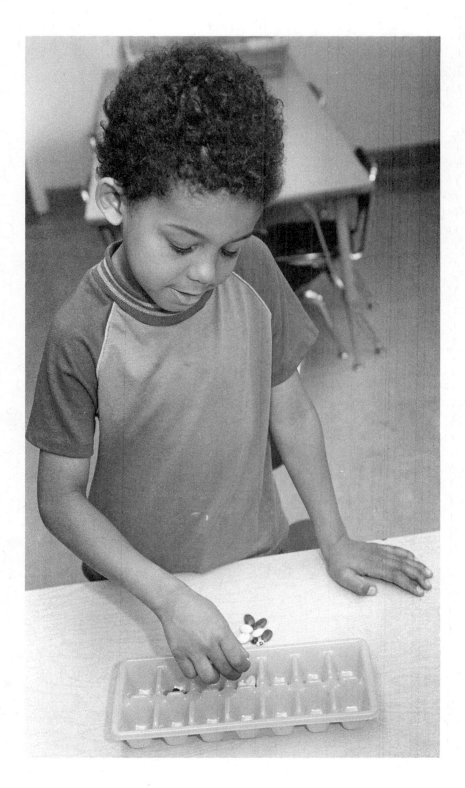

Science Concept

Plants have a great diversity of physical characteristics.

Science Process Skill

To use observations to classify objects into groups.

Science Vocabulary

descriptive words for seeds
left
right
seeds
seed names

ACTIVITY 4

Which Is Strongest?

Materials

herbs, both fresh and dried, such as basil, chives, dill, and parsley
large sheet of newsprint
paper plates
tape or glue
scissors

Children's food choices are often influenced by the way foods smell and taste. In this activity the children will explore fresh and dried herbs and compare the strengths of their odors. When used in cooking, dried herbs are usually two to three times stronger than fresh herbs in both smell and taste. Fresh herbs, however, will usually smell stronger before cooking than dried herbs.

Before the Activity

Make a Which Is Strongest? Discovery Chart. Rinse the fresh herbs and place each sample on a plate along with a sample of the dried herb.

What to Do

1. Give each group a pair of herbs. Ask the children to observe the herbs.

2. Ask: Which smells stronger, the fresh herb or the dry herb? Odors may be mild to overpowering in strength; encourage the children to use their creativity to describe what they smell. You may want to show the children how to crush the leaves to release more odor from the herbs.

C·O·N·N·E·C·T·I·O·N·S

To Language

Expressive Language - Children will use their creativity to describe what they smell.

To Math

Charting - Children will use a chart to organize and communicate their impressions of the odors.

3. Have the children tape or glue a sample of the fresh and the dried herb into a pair of boxes on the Which Is Strongest? Discovery Chart. Then have them mark which of the two smells the strongest.

4. Send home Plants Family Connection Activity 3 (page 291).

Assessing the Activity

Discuss the completed Discovery Chart with the children. Do they clearly understand why herbs are located on the Fresh or Dried side of the Chart? Hold up a dried and a fresh herb, and ask the children on which side of the chart these samples should be placed. Do the children understand why the herbs are marked (to indicate strength)? Pass a final pair of herbs around the group, and ask the children to vote on which sample has the strongest odor.

Science Concept

Plants have a great diversity of physical characteristics.

Science Process Skill

To use observations to classify objects into groups.

Science Vocabulary

dried
fresh
herbs
odor
strong
weak

Which Is Strongest?

Fresh	Dried

ACTIVITY 5

Leaves Have Veins Too

Materials

an assortment of leaves

Leaf Veins chart

thick telephone books, catalogs, or plant press for drying leaves

magnifying glasses

Discovery Journals

Leaves have veins; people have veins. Leaf veins supply water and minerals to the leaf cells; people's veins carry blood and nutrients throughout their bodies. The children will classify the vein patterns of the leaves by three types of vein patterns: pinnate, palmate, and parallel. Veins are a primary classification tool for botanists.

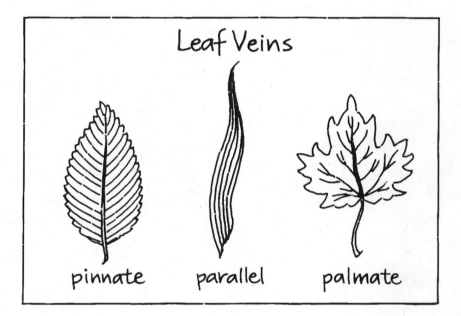

Leaf Veins

pinnate   parallel   palmate

C▪O▪N▪N▪E▪C▪T▪I▪O▪N▪S

To Language

Expressive Language - Children will make comparisons between veins in the human body and veins in leaves.

To Math

Comparing - Children will compare the veins in their leaves to the vein patterns shown on the Leaf Veins chart.

Science Concept

Plants have a great diversity of physical characteristics.

Science Process Skill

To use observations to classify objects into groups.

Science Vocabulary

palmate
parallel
pinnate
plant names
veins

Before the Activity

Prepare the Leaf Veins chart. Collect leaves to supplement the children's collection. Request that the children bring a few tree leaves from home. Tell them to pick only one leaf per tree.

What to Do

1. Let the children place one of their leaves into a book or a plant press to dry. Drying will take about a week, depending on the humidity.

2. Ask: Do you know what veins are? Do you have veins? What do they do? Do leaves have veins? Distribute the remaining leaves.

3. Have the children examine the leaves by holding them up to the light and using magnifying glasses. Suggest that they focus on vein patterns. Ask: How are the vein patterns different? Have them look at the Leaf Veins chart to classify their leaves, and trace or draw their leaves in their Discovery Journals.

Assessing the Activity

Can the children match their leaves to the appropriate vein pattern on the Leaf Veins chart?

CHECKPOINT

How Do They Look?

Materials

assortment of seeds (see Before the Activity) in an open container such as a baking pan

small paper plates (1 per pair)

5 to 8 sheets of construction paper

clear tape

chalkboard or large sheet of newsprint

Discovery Journals

This activity will provide a flexible means for assessing the children's understanding of simple classification. The children will develop their own set of categories and will classify seeds accordingly.

Before the Activity

Have seeds of different colors, textures, and sizes. For example, large seeds such as beans, corn, peas, and squash; and small seeds such as radishes, lettuce, and carrots.

What to Do

1. Children may work in pairs for this activity. Ask each pair to choose some seeds and to place them on a paper plate.

2. Ask: What are some ways seeds are alike? Different? What are some words that describe your seeds? How do they look? How do they feel? List their words on the chalkboard or newsprint.

C·O·N·N·E·C·T·I·O·N·S

To Language

Expressive Language - Children will describe how seeds are alike and different, using a variety of descriptive categories.

Written Language - Children will write or dictate descriptive words for seeds.

To Math

Classifying - Children will develop a classification system for seeds that allows them to place seeds in separate categories.

Science Concept

Plants have a great diversity of physical characteristics.

Science Process Skill

To use observations to classify objects into groups.

Science Vocabulary

classify
descriptive words for seed colors, textures, shapes, and sizes
seeds

3. With the children, select five to eight descriptive categories, such as light, dark, round, flat, rough, and smooth. If the children suggest several color words, such as brown, black, white, and red, help them understand that light and dark would be broader categories. Write the selected words on construction paper, one word per sheet.

4. Hold up one piece of construction paper and read the word; for example, *Big*. Direct the pairs who have what they consider to be a big seed to tape their seeds on the page. Continue until all the seeds have been classified.

5. Discuss the fact that many seeds could have been placed in several categories. Can they find examples in which this happened? For example, someone might have placed a watermelon seed on the *Dark* page, while another child put it on the *Smooth* page.

6. Have the children choose seeds to tape in their Discovery Journals. Ask: What words can you write or tell me to describe this seed? Write dictated descriptions if requested to do so. Some children will want to write their own words.

Assessing the Activity

Observe the children as they categorize their seeds. Are they accurate? Do the words in their Discovery Journals describe the seeds?

ADDITIONAL STIMULATION

Leaf Prints

Materials

assortment of leaves that are still moist and flexible (1 per child)

several pieces of plywood or particle board

white or pastel bed sheets torn into 15-by-15-cm squares (1 per child)

several mallets or small hammers

newspapers (optional)

Collecting fall leaves is a common school activity. However, you can collect some sort of leaves almost any time of the year.

Before the Activity

Take the children on a walk to collect an assortment of leaves. Take leaves from a variety of trees. Collect only one leaf from each tree.

What to Do

1. Have each child choose one leaf. Show the children how to place the leaf on the board, cover it with a piece of cloth, and pound it with the hammer until the print appears on the cloth. You might want to place a stack of newspapers under the board to absorb sound.

2. As the children complete the prints, have them set the prints aside to dry.

C▪O▪N▪N▪E▪C▪T▪I▪O▪N▪S

To Language

Expressive Language - Children will describe how leaf prints are alike and different, using a variety of descriptive categories such as shape, color, shading, and vein patterns.

To Math

Classifying - Children will develop a classification system for the leaves that allows them to place them in separate categories.

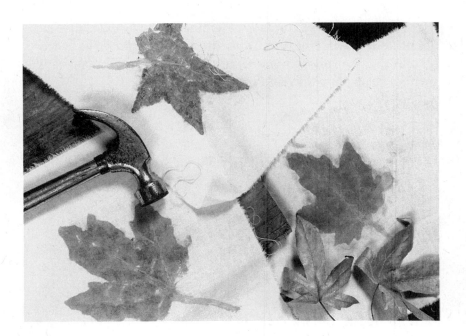

Science Concept

Plants have a great diversity of physical characteristics.

Science Process Skill

To use observations to classify objects into groups.

Science Vocabulary

classify
descriptive words for leaf colors, shapes, and sizes
stain
vein

3. After the prints have dried, ask the children to sort the prints into groups showing similar kinds of leaves. They may choose to classify by size, shape, color, or some other attribute.

Assessing the Activity

Observe the children as they categorize the leaf prints. Do they suggest reasonable categories for classification? Are they accurate? Are they able to group them in more than one way?

ACTIVITY 1

What Plant Did You Eat?

Materials

Discovery Journals

Some of the foods we eat daily originate from plants. Children are not often aware of this. Many of them may think the grocery store is the one and only source of food. This activity will enable them to focus on plants as a food source.

C▪O▪N▪N▪E▪C▪T▪I▪O▪N▪S

To Language

Expressive Language - Children will talk about the foods they ate recently, as well as their conception of where the foods came from.

Written Language - Children will label the plants they draw at their own developmental level.

Science Concept

Plants have a great diversity of physical characteristics.

Science Process Skill

To organize and communicate observations.

Science Vocabulary

compare
plant foods
plant names
plant part names

What to Do

1. Ask the children what they ate the day before. Ask them to draw pictures of the foods in their Discovery Journals.

2. Ask: How many of the foods that you ate came from plants? Have the children circle the drawings of foods they think came from plants.

3. As a class, talk about the foods that are circled. Identify whether each indeed came from a plant, and from what parts of plants they came from. (For example, a carrot is a root, lettuce is leaves, broccoli is a stem and flower, an apple is a fruit, and peas are seeds.)

4. Ask the children to draw pictures in their Discovery Journals of a favorite food that comes from a plant. Have them label the drawings at their own developmental level.

Assessing the Activity

Observe the drawings. Do they represent foods that come from plants? Can the children tell you which plant their foods come from?

ACTIVITY 2

Neighborhood Plant Walk

Materials

Discovery Journals

This activity will give the children an opportunity to observe plants they find growing in environments other than the classroom and to draw them from memory.

What to Do

1. Take the children on a walk in a nearby neighborhood.

2. Ask them to point out the plants they observe growing in this environment.

3. Do not hurry this activity. Tell the children to look closely at the plants and to describe what they see in detail.

4. When you return to the classroom, suggest that the children draw in their Discovery Journals some of the plants they saw. Encourage them to make their own captions or dictate words to you.

5. Send home Plants Family Connection Activity 4 (page 291).

C▪O▪N▪N▪E▪C▪T▪I▪O▪N▪S

To Language

Expressive Language - Children will discuss and describe the variety of plants that they observe during a plant walk.

Discovery Journals - Children will draw some plants they saw during a plant walk and label the drawings at their own ability level.

Science Concept

Plants have a great diversity of physical characteristics.

Science Process Skill

To organize and communicate observations.

Science Vocabulary

plant names
plant parts and other descriptive terms

Assessing the Activity

The drawings and the verbal exchanges will be an indication of the children's ability to observe real plants and their characteristics and to communicate these observations to others.

ACTIVITY 3

Let's Plan a Garden

Materials

garden spot or window boxes
variety of seeds
small wooden stakes (such as tongue depressors)
ruler
planting tools
string
Discovery Journals

In this activity the children will plan a garden as a group and then record in their own Discovery Journals what will be grown. If an outdoor garden is not an option, consider planting one or more window boxes.

Before the Activity

Prepare the garden spot or window boxes for planting. This will include turning the soil, hoeing, and raking. You might have the children help you.

What to Do

1. Discuss with the children what they might plant in the garden. Talk about how much space is needed for different kinds of plants. Allow them to choose what they'd like to grow from the variety of the seeds you offer them.

C ▪ O ▪ N ▪ N ▪ E ▪ C ▪ T ▪ I ▪ O ▪ N ▪ S

To Language

Expressive Language - Children will engage in active discussion as they decide what to plant in a garden.

Discovery Journals - Children will make sketches of the garden and label them at their ability levels.

To Math

Counting and Measuring - Children will use counting and measuring skills as they plan their garden.

Science Concept

Plants are living organisms that require water, light, and nourishment for growth and survival.

Science Process Skill

To organize and communicate observations.

Science Vocabulary

garden
grid
plan
plant names
plot

2. In the area to be planted, use the wooden stakes and string to lay out rows. Talk about what will be planted in each row. On each wooden stake attach a picture of the plant to be planted in that row (seeds packets are good for this purpose) or write the name of the type of plant. Keep the plan simple; use three or four different plants.

3. Let the children plant the seeds.

4. Have the children draw in their Discovery Journals the general shape of the garden plot and label the rows at their ability level.

Assessing the Activity

Check the children's Discovery Journal entries for both row location and accuracy of labels.

CHECKPOINT

My Plant Poster

Materials

large sheets of paper (1 per child)

picture of the selected plant (classroom photos or cut by the children from seed catalogs)

dried plant parts (optional)

scissors

tape, paste, or glue

Discovery Journals

This activity provides a way for the children to pull together observational, data collection, and organizational skills in a personalized way. They are asked to find one plant among all those the class has explored and focus on it. To tell about their plants, they will create posters that can later be displayed for everyone to see.

Before the Activity

Collect a number of seed and plant catalogs. Ask parents to help.

What to Do

1. Ask the children to select a plant that they would like to make a poster about. You may want to suggest a plant or even develop a class poster as an example.

2. Have the children use classroom photographs or find pictures of their plant in catalogues to put on the poster. Children can substitute drawings if pictures are not available.

3. Have children tape or paste the pictures on the poster. If available, dried parts of real plants—leaves, twigs, dried flowers—can be added.

C ▪ O ▪ N ▪ N ▪ E ▪ C ▪ T ▪ I ▪ O ▪ N ▪ S

To Language

Expressive Language - Children will exhibit their expanded science and descriptive vocabulary as they talk about the plants they have chosen.

Science Concept

Plants are living organisms that require water, light, and nourishment for growth and survival.

Science Process Skill

To organize and communicate observations.

Science Vocabulary

plant names
words to describe plant parts, seeds, size, shape, and color

4. Ask the children to describe the way a plant looks using all the words they have learned as they observed plants during the Plants unit. Have them write these words themselves or dictate them to you.

Assessing the Activity

The poster should be representative of the knowledge each child has gained through the experiences in the Plants unit. Poster entries may be checked for accuracy of labels, descriptions, and vocabulary. Look for the children's understanding and ability to organize and communicate information regarding their plant choice.

ADDITIONAL STIMULATION

Seed Detective

Materials

large sheet of paper or tag board

collection of seeds

scissors

paste or glue

basket or other container

clear tape

small cards, such as cut-up index cards

In this activity children are asked to go beyond the classroom to create a set of seeds. The children will develop their communication skills by using the set to describe and match seed pairs. The activity's two phases give the children observational time followed by a communication activity.

Before the Activity

Have children bring from home seeds from plants, such as watermelon, grapefruit, apple, avocado, acorns, orange, peach, walnut, date, grass, rice, peas, beans, chestnuts, cantaloupe, pine cones, maple, and palmetto. The greater the variety the better. You will need at least two of each seed type. Ask parents to help. Also collect a number of seeds you think the children might not bring in. Go for a seed walk on the schools grounds or through the neighborhood. Spices provide many strange seeds with another sensory attribute, smell.

What to Do

1. Bring the seeds together into one big collection. Let the children organize the seed collection into like pairs, glue each seed onto a card, tape one card from each pair on the chart, and place the other cards in the basket.

C ▪ O ▪ N ▪ N ▪ E ▪ C ▪ T ▪ I ▪ O ▪ N ▪ S

To Language

Expressive Language - Children will describe how seeds are alike and different along with such characteristics as size, shape, color, texture, and appearance.

To Math

Comparing - Children will use comparative language as they talk about their selected plants.

Classifying - Children will develop a classification system for seeds on the seed chart.

2. Place the chart on the wall in an accessible place and the basket of cards on the floor below the chart.

3. Ask groups or pairs of children to take a seed card and to match the seed with its pair on the chart. As the match is made, have the children describe why it is a match.

4. When the children are familiar with the seeds and with the descriptive words for them, have one or two children describe the seed for another child or group of children to find on the chart.

Assessing the Activity

Observe the children as they organize and communicate their information. The clearer the use of descriptive words by the children, the easier the partners will find the seed pair.

THE FAMILY CONNECTION

This section includes a complete plan for setting up and running your own Discovery Science Family Night to introduce families to the Discovery Science curriculum, philosophy, goals, and activities. It also includes samples of letters you might send home with the children at the beginning of each unit to explain what the children will be exploring and to ask for help and donations of materials. The letters invite families to participate in the Family Connection activities, contained in plastic bags of materials the children will periodically bring home to extend their science experiences. For each Family Connection activity, put the materials called for and a photocopy of the instructions in plastic resealable bags.

Discovery Science Family Night

Dear Family,

This year we will be using a program designed to introduce your child to the exciting world of science. The program is called Discovery Science, and it is just that. It enables children to learn science through discovery—through *interactions* with materials. In other words, they will be learning science the way we all learn best: by doing, exploring, asking questions, and finding answers.

This letter is an invitation to you to come and learn what Discovery Science is all about and what you can do at home to extend this exciting learning experience for your child. The meeting will last for an hour and a half. You will have the opportunity to try many activities that you can do with your child at home. By the close of the meeting, you will have an understanding of the philosophy, goals, and activities of Discovery Science.

I want you to be comfortable, so please dress casually. I promise to start and finish on time. We will have refreshments. Because this is an "adults only" meeting, child care will be provided.

The meeting will be held at _____ on _____ from _____ to _____ . If you are able to attend, please return the bottom of this letter. Let me know how many adults will be coming and whether you need child care.

I look forward to doing Discovery Science with you.

Sincerely,

Please Detach and Return

_____ adults will attend the Discovery Science meeting.

_____ children, ages _____ , will need child care.

Name _____

Reminder Flier

FAMILY

MEETING

DISCOVERY SCIENCE FAMILY MEETING

DISCOVERY SCIENCE

INFORMAL
DRESS

CHILD CARE
PROVIDED

A FAMILY MEETING

THAT PROMISES TO TURN YOU ON

TO SCIENCE!

Where _____

Date _____

Time _____

REFRESHMENTS PROVIDED

Name Tag and Mixer

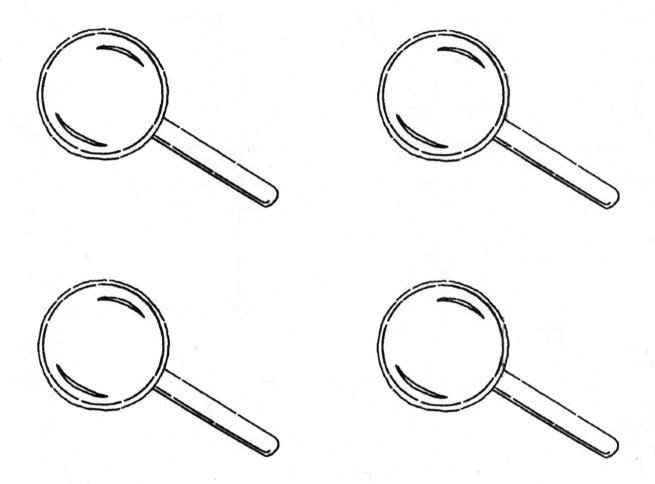

MIXER PROCEDURE

Trace the pattern on colored construction paper and cut out the magnifying glasses. Write a number from 1 to 4 on each handle. This number will assign each family member to one of the four activity centers.

As people arrive, hand them a name tag and a pin. Ask that they write their name on the tag and then find another person or persons with the same color of tag. Ask them to introduce themselves and to talk about how they learned science when they were in school and how they felt about it—then and now.

Sample Agenda for Planning a Family Night

Purpose: To introduce families to the Discovery Science curriculum, philosophy, goals, and activities.

Three Weeks Before Meeting

1. Clear meeting with principal.
2. Secure authorization for room use.
3. Secure room for child care.
4. Make arrangements for several child-care providers, on standby, depending on the number of children coming.
5. Form a committee to make transportation arrangements for families who need rides.
6. Set up a refreshment committee with chairperson. Post food sign-up list.

Two Weeks Before Meeting

1. Prepare and send invitations.
2. Lay out the physical arrangement of the room on paper.
3. Decide which Family Connection activities will be used for hands-on experience. Choose at least one activity from each of the four units.

One Week Before Meeting

1. Prepare name tags.
2. Prepare evaluation form and "The Role of the Family" handout.
3. Prepare Family Connection Kits for the activities you have chosen.
4. Check with refreshment committee chairperson. Remind families of foods they signed up to bring.
5. Send home reminder flier with each child.

One Day Before Meeting

1. Send home final reminder.
2. Check progress of refreshment committee. Get final head count.
3. Remind child-care providers of date and time. Be sure you have enough people for the age and number of children coming.
4. Check with transportation committee to verify rides for families needing them.

Day of Meeting

1. Set up chairs. Set up tables for the four Family Connection activity centers, and mark the centers 1, 2, 3, and 4.
2. Put up signs directing families to meeting location.
3. Put name tags and Family Connection Kits in place.

Sample Family Meeting Plan

Time	Activity	Technique	Resources/Materials
7:00 – 7:10	Welcome	Name tags, mixer	Name tags, markers, pins
7:10 – 7:30	Introduction to Discovery Science and the Family Connection	Seat families in circle. Mini-lecture.	Introduction to Discovery Science, pages 1–19
7:30 – 8:00	Families go to four activity centers	Explain each of the centers and how families might interact with their child while doing the activities. Have them begin at the center that matches the number on their name tag and rotate to visit all of the centers. Move throughout the room suggesting possible adult/child interactions.	Family Connection activities, at least one per table
8:00 – 8:15	Families return to large group	Wrap up. Present "The Role of the Family" and hand out copies.	Handout: "The Role of the Family"
8:15 – 8:30	Conclusion and refreshments	Hand out evaluation forms. Serve refreshments.	Evaluation forms, pencils

The Role of the Family

- To encourage discovery by the children.
- To model inquiry and problem solving.
- To resist answering and solving discovery activities before the child has done so.
- To enjoy doing science activities with the child.
- To feel free to communicate with the child's teacher, to ask questions, and to seek additional information when needed.
- To listen to and give information to the child, always remembering that it is all right for any participant to make mistakes or to say, "I don't know."
- To willingly share available resources from home, such as animals, plants, or soil samples, to be used for Discovery Science activities.

The Role of the Family

- To encourage discovery by the children.
- To model inquiry and problem solving.
- To resist answering and solving discovery activities before the child has done so.
- To enjoy doing science activities with the child.
- To feel free to communicate with the child's teacher, to ask questions, and to seek additional information when needed.
- To listen to and give information to the child, always remembering that it is all right for any participant to make mistakes or to say, "I don't know."
- To willingly share available resources from home, such as animals, plants, or soil samples, to be used for Discovery Science activities.

Family Meeting Evaluation

I am interested in knowing whether you enjoyed the meeting this evening. Please put a check under the magnifying glass that best describes your feelings about the meeting. The space at the bottom of this page is for any questions or suggestions you might have. I would be happy to hear from you, so please feel free to comment.

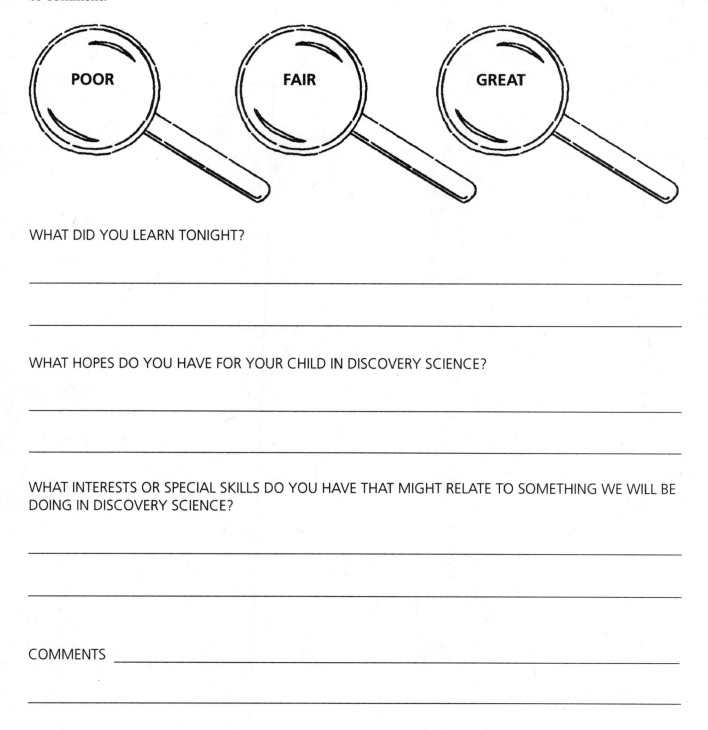

WHAT DID YOU LEARN TONIGHT?

_____

_____

WHAT HOPES DO YOU HAVE FOR YOUR CHILD IN DISCOVERY SCIENCE?

_____

_____

WHAT INTERESTS OR SPECIAL SKILLS DO YOU HAVE THAT MIGHT RELATE TO SOMETHING WE WILL BE DOING IN DISCOVERY SCIENCE?

_____

_____

COMMENTS _____

_____

Family Letters and Family Connection Activities

Use these sample letters to write your own family letters announcing each unit. Copy and cut apart the Family Connection activity slips. Send the slips, along with the indicated materials, home with the children at the appropriate times during each unit.

Magnets

Dear Family,

Next week your child and I will begin the Magnets unit of Discovery Science. We will be exploring magnets for the next several weeks. I want to invite you to take part in this experience by becoming involved with our work with magnets.

The children will be bringing home some interesting activities to share with their families. We call these materials Family Connection activities. Each activity is enclosed in a resealable plastic packet. The packet includes materials for the activity and information about what the children will do. Be prepared to repeat the activity over and over as your child shares the excitement of Discovery Science. These packets should be returned to the school in two days with comments from you and your child.

Please remember to let your child show you and tell you what he or she has learned. Letting your child teach you is a great way to make it known that you think what your child is learning is important.

If you have games or materials that use magnets and would be willing to share them with the class for a few days, please bring them to school or send them with your child. If you have any questions or would like to help in any way, please send a note or call me. Thank you so much for your support and interest in Discovery Science for your child.

Sincerely,

Magnets Family Connection Activity 1

For use with
Can You Stop a Magnet?

Materials
magnet
paper clip

What to Do

You and your child will be investigating how many things you can find in your home that magnetic force can pass through.

1. Have your child show you how we tested materials at school. (We held a magnet on one side of a material, such as cardboard, and a paper clip on the other side to see if the magnet attracted the paper clip through the material.)

2. Now test materials in your home. You might try fabric, plastic wrap, glass, or a door.

3. If you wish, you and your child may send me a sentence or two about what you discovered.

Magnets Family Connection Activity 2

For use with
Bouncing Magnets

Materials
2 painted donut-shaped magnets
plastic straw

What to Do

1. Have your child show you how we made magnets bounce at school.

2. Now put a magnet on the straw. Have your child put on the second magnet. What happens? Can your child find a way to make the magnets bounce every time?

3. If you wish, write down your child's "rule" for making the magnets bounce. He or she may bring it to school when returning the kit.

Magnets Family Connection Activity 3

For use with
Yes or No, the Magnet Knows

Materials
magnet

What to Do

1. Walk through your home. In each room have your child predict which items will be attracted by a magnet. Make a list of these items as your child identifies them. Please do not make any comments about right or wrong predictions.

2. Now take a second journey through your home. Have your child use the magnet to check the predictions.

3. If you like, you and your child may send me the list of predictions and answers.

Magnets Family Connection Activity 4

For use with
Refrigerator Fun

Materials
magnet
pieces of paper

What to Do

1. Have your child use the magnet to hold one piece of paper on the refrigerator.

2. Try more sheets of paper. Ask you child: How many pieces of paper will the magnet hold?

3. If you have other magnets at home, you may want to test them and compare them with the magnet your child brought home.

Rocks and Soil

Dear Family,

Next week your child and I will begin the Rocks and Soil unit of Discovery Science. I want to invite you to participate by doing the Family Connection activities that your child will be bringing home over the next few weeks.

Please let me know if you have anything that you could lend the class for the unit. I am looking for rock collections, unusual items made from rocks such as arrowheads or carvings, and any other unusual rocks the children might find interesting.

If you collect rocks, we would enjoy having you visit to share your hobby. If you know someone who is a jeweler or who works in some capacity with rocks or soil, please tell him or her about the unit and that I am seeking volunteers to share information with the children. I welcome any contribution of time or talent.

If you have any questions or can help in any way, please send me a note or call me. Thank you so much for your support and continued interest in your child's Discovery Science.

Sincerely,

Rocks and Soil Family Connection Activity 1

For use with
Not All Rocks Look Alike

Materials
a rock the child selected in class

What to Do

1. Have your child tell you all about his or her rock.

2. See whether your child can find other rocks that are similar. Look in driveways, creek beds, quarries, or beaches.

3. If you find any rocks that are very interesting, have your child tell you all about what makes them special.

4. Have your child draw a picture of the special rock. With your child, write about the rock. Your child may want to bring the picture to school when he or she returns the kit.

Rocks and Soil Family Connection Activity 2

For use with
Do You See the Rock I See?

Materials
several rocks

What to Do

1. Your child has learned an interesting chant in school. It goes like this: I see a rock, and it is _____ [describe one of the rocks, using words like round, dark, and flat]. Do you know which rock I see?

2. When you feel comfortable with the chant, you and your child can take turns until all of the rocks have been identified.

Rocks and Soil Family Connection Activity 3

For use with
It's All Wet

Materials
small plastic cup
toothpicks
dropper
clay soil sample

Your child has been learning about what happens when water and soil are mixed.

What to Do

1. Have your child place a small amount of the soil into the cup, then add drops of water until the soil holds together like cookie dough.

2. Have your child use this moistened soil to mold a figure (for example, an animal or a person). Allow it to dry.

3. Have your child tell you what has happened to the soil as water was added. Ask what happened as it dried.

4. If you and your child desire, you may smash the figure and return it to its original form. Repeat the process as many times as you would like. Your child may bring a figure back to school to share with the class.

Rocks and Soil Family Connection Activity 4

For use with
Which Rock Is the Longest?

Materials
rocks
several interlocking cubes

What to Do

1. Look at the rock with your child. Have your child guess how many cubes long the rock is. Write down the guesses.

2. Use the cubes to measure the rock with your child to see whether the guesses were correct.

3. Find other rocks to measure with the cubes.

Animals

Dear Family,

Next week your child and I will begin the Animals unit of Discovery Science. We will be exploring animals for the next several weeks. Your child will develop an understanding of animals and also abilities to nurture and care for them.

Two outstanding features of this unit are the One-Week Zoo and the long-term classroom residents. During the One-Week Zoo, children are given the opportunity to interact intensively with a variety of animals, such as hamsters, guinea pigs, box turtles, garden snakes, birds, and snails. The long-term classroom residents are animals that will remain in the classroom for the duration of the Animals unit or longer. These might be crickets, worms, gerbils, a rabbit, or ants in an ant farm.

We will need animals for both of these experiences. We also will need cages, feeders, aquariums, and appropriate animal food. If you have an animal that you are willing to lend us for a day, a week, or longer, please contact me or send a note with your child.

This should be an exciting unit both at school and at home. I will be sending Family Connection activities for this unit. As you do the activities with your child, be prepared to listen as well as to give information. Remember that it is okay for both of you to make mistakes and to say, "I don't know."

Thank you for your support and interest in the children's Discovery Science.

Sincerely,

Animals Family Connection Activity 1

For use with
Animals and the Senses

Materials
set of sense cards (see page 137)

What to Do

1. Select one of the cards and show it to your child.
2. Have your child tell for what sense the picture on the card stands.
3. Ask: What are you noticing with that sense right now?
4. If you have a pet, see whether you and your child can observe it using any of its senses.
5. If you like, you and your child may send me a sentence or two about what you observed.

Animals Family Connection Activity 2

For use with
Alike and Different

Materials
animal pictures from magazines

What to Do

1. Ask your child to tell you what animal is in the picture. Have your child describe the animal.
2. Look at some magazines or books together and find pictures of other animals. Ask your child how these animals are alike or different from the one in the pictures they brought home.
3. If you wish, send me a sentence or two about the similarities and differences your child noticed. We will share these comments in class.

Animals Family Connection Activity 3

For use with
Animal Odds and Ends

Materials
resealable plastic bag (numbered) with a few small items from the Animal Discovery Collection

What to Do

1. Take the items out of the bag and look at them. Can you and your child figure out what animals the objects came from?
2. Write down the number on the bag and list the animals that you and your child think the items came from. An "I don't have a clue!" answer is just fine.
3. If you have something to add to our collection, please send it to school with your child.

Animals Family Connection Activity 4

For use with
What Does Our Animal Smell?

Materials
set of scent bags (resealable bags, each containing a cotton ball with a different scent such as vinegar, lemon, peppermint, pine, orange, and vanilla)

What to Do

1. Have your child ask you (and other family members) to smell one bag at a time and tell what you think of the smell.
2. Help your child keep a simple record of which smells were liked and disliked. Your child may bring this to school when returning the kit.

Plants

Dear Family,

Next week your child and I will be starting the final unit in Discovery Science—Plants. We will be exploring plants for several weeks as the children learn about plant characteristics, plant variety, and the ways plants are used.

Once again I will be sending Family Connection activities home with your child. Be sure to resist answering and solving the activities for your child. It is important for your child to make independent discoveries.

As in the previous units, I am asking your help in providing resources for the children. I will need house plants (real and artificial), assorted seeds, herbs (dried or fresh), potting soil, sand, and planting containers.

I am also in need of volunteers who can share information about flower or vegetable gardening. If you know a flower wholesaler, florist, or greenhouse tender, we certainly would enjoy having that person share his or her expertise with us.

If you have any questions or can help in any way, please send a note or call me. Thank you so much for your help in making science an exciting and rewarding experience for your child.

Sincerely,

Plants Family Connection Activity 1

For use with
Leaf Rubbings

Materials
crayons without paper wrappings
pieces of paper

What to Do

1. Take a leaf-collecting walk with your child. Look for a variety of shapes and sizes, including the leaves of weeds.

2. Make a rubbing of a leaf. Your child can show you how to do this. Place a leaf under a piece of paper and rub with the side of a crayon. Then you and your child may make rubbings of all the leaves you collected.

3. Talk about the variety of leaves you found and the shapes of the rubbings. Are some of the shapes similar to each other?

4. Have your child bring a rubbing to school when returning the kit to show the class what kind of leaves are in your area.

Plants Family Connection Activity 2

For use with
Seeds or Nonseeds: Which Grow Better?

Materials
small packets of grass seed; nonseed material (buttons, small twigs, etc.); and potting soil
2 small paper cups

What to Do

1. Let your child fill the two cups with soil and plant grass seed in one and the nonseed material in the other.

2. Place the containers in a warm location and water as needed. Ask your child to predict what will happen.

3. Talk about the results when the grass begins to grow. Compare the containers. (There is no need to return this kit.)

Plants Family Connection Activity 3

For use with
Which Is Strongest?

Materials
small packets of oregano, dill, and chives, or other herbs

What to Do

1. Help your child put a small amount of butter or cream cheese into each of three separate containers. Add one type of herb to each container. Mix each well.

2. Spread the mixtures on toast or crackers.

3. Eat and decide which you like. Do you and your child agree?

4. If you wish, you and your child may send me a sentence or two about how you liked this activity.

Plants Family Connection Activity 4

For use with
Neighborhood Plant Walk

Materials
pencil
paper

What to Do

1. Take your child on a walk around the neighborhood.

2. Ask your child to point out plants. As your child points out a plant, list it on the paper. If you do not know the name, write a description ("the one with scratchy leaves" or "the one with little purple flowers"). Let your child make up the description.

3. When you get back home, talk about the many plants that you have listed.

4. Let your child make a drawing of his or her favorite plant to bring to school.